PEBBLE BEACH
to
AUGUSTA

PEBBLE BEACH
to
AUGUSTA

One Man's Journey to
Play the World's
Top 100 Courses

by
LEON WENTZ
with Jerry Stewart

A Mountain Lion Book

ISBN 0-9770039-1-4

Pebble Beach®, Pebble Beach Golf Links®, Spyglass Hill®
Golf Course, and their respective underlying distinctive
images are trademarks, service marks, and trade dress
of Pebble Beach Company. Used under license.

Jacket and text design by Bob Antler
Antler Designworks

Pebble Beach to Augusta:
One Man's Journey to Play the World's Top 100 Courses
is available at special quantity discounts for use as premiums
and sales promotions, or for use in corporate golf outings.
For more information, please contact:

John Monteleone at Mountain Lion, Inc.,
P.O. Box 799, Pennington, NJ 08534,
609-730-1665, 609-468-2661, 609-730-1286 (fax),
or jmontel738@aol.com

*I've always been a believer that
one has to follow his or her dreams.*

Through the support of many individuals, directly and indirectly, I was able to complete a journey that consisted of playing the Top 100 golf courses in the world. The networking and travel were at times challenging, but with the support and encouragement of many others I was able to complete my goal.

Specifically, I would like to dedicate this book to my parents, who enjoyed golf so much, my lovely wife Cathy, who was my cheerleader for eight years, and the many enablers worldwide, who are recognized in the Acknowledgments section. Of course, this dedication is also to the game of golf, which regretfully I started all too late in life.

In celebrating golf, I have decided that all net proceeds from this book will benefit The First Tee, a national nonprofit organization whose mission is to impact the lives of young people by providing learning facilities and educational programs that promote character development and life-enhancing values through the game of golf.

*I hope you will enjoy the journey.
I certainly did.*

Contents

Contents

Introduction

After eight excruciating and exhilarating years, my quest was nearly over.

On April 26, 2005, I was scheduled to tee off at 10 a.m. on the hallowed ground that is Augusta National Golf Club, home of the world-renowned Masters tournament.

I couldn't have been more eager and excited about following in the footsteps of legendary golfers Bobby Jones, Arnold Palmer and Jack Nicklaus. However, the Georgia weatherman had other ideas. It was raining and I was sitting in my car outside Augusta's gated entrance, watching the clock tick down and the dark clouds roll in.

Soon, the rain began playing a dirge, intermittently interrupted by booming claps of thunder. I raised my eyes to the skies, looking and hoping for a break in the clouds. No blue skies, no white, puffy clouds in sight. What bad luck—this was supposed to be my day, the opportunity I'd been waiting for, dreaming about, fighting for.

Eight years earlier, at age 60, I had decided to take on what I thought would be the ultimate quest in golf: I would play the World's Top 100 Golf Courses, as compiled by *Golf Magazine*. The rankings had changed four times since I began my quest but I never wavered from my goal: to conquer the latest list. I'd played 99 courses of the Top 100 and I needed only to play Augusta National to make 100.

Along the way I'd met hundreds of fascinating people, including a leather-faced Scottish caddie who had a penchant for drinking Scotch and chain-smoking, a prominent Japanese businessman who graciously offered me the services of his limousine, and a club captain at a course in England who broke a 107-year golf club tradition just for me.

I'd encountered hazards on and off the golf courses. At Muirfield Golf Club in Scotland, I played on crutches, and at a course in South Africa, I had to fend off monkeys. At Bethpage Black Course in New York, I spent the wee hours of the morning waiting in a parking lot for a tee-time. In New Zealand, I had the surprise of playing in a pro-am tournament and the shock of a dental emergency.

At times the quest slowed or paused but in my mind it never ceased edging forward. When I wasn't traveling and playing I was planning and dreaming. Now my dream was only 18 holes from realization.

I fidgeted with the dial on the car radio, looking for an updated weather report. Suddenly I felt a pit in my stomach, and a shattering thought flashed through my mind. This defining day and my round might be washed out, and who knew when, if ever, I'd be able to reschedule the final round of my quest?

I reflected briefly about how a sniff of the mystique and history of famous golf courses such as Augusta National, Pine Valley, Royal Melbourne, St. Andrews, Pebble Beach, and Cypress Point can intoxicate you and perhaps even turn a quest into an obsession. A grand quest or magnificent obsession, it really didn't matter. At this moment, I simply wanted to pass through that gate and play Augusta National Golf Club.

I had already accomplished plenty in life. In my career as a builder, I had worked my way from constructing small projects to witnessing hundreds of my visions come to life as major buildings and infrastructures. I had raised three fantastic children, was succeeding as a doting grandfather, and was happily married to my second wife, Cathy.

Just prior to undertaking my quest I'd lost my first wife, Jeanie, and since had battled prostate cancer and peripheral neuropathy, an affliction that numbs the nerves in one's feet.

Amidst the sound of my windshield wipers' rhythmic slapping my mind again wandered, revisiting my fears: What if my member-host never showed up because of the inclement weather? Would I ever find another way to access the course? Is my quest going to end at 99 courses?

For a fleeting moment, I entertained the idea of sneaking onto the course. According to reports, one enterprising soul built a raft, gathered up his buddies and floated onto the grounds via Rae's Creek. Others had hidden inside trunks of cars. I had to laugh. Who was I kidding? My days of hopping fences were long gone, and I wasn't about to play Rambo. If I was to complete my quest, I couldn't play Augusta National as an interloper. I was going to do it the right way.

I had arrived an hour earlier than the appointed

time, and the arrival time of my host was yet another 30 minutes away. I turned off the crackling radio, cut the swishing windshield wipers, and sat quietly listening to the pelting rain, all the while growing more and more anxious as the appointed time approached, doubting and wondering if I'd ever get that thumbs-up from the security guard, the signal that the grand finale of my unique golf odyssey across five continents was about to commence.

Suddenly a car pulled up alongside me.

The driver was my host. He stepped out of the car, came over, introduced himself, and said, like an angel, "Follow me."

As I followed his car down historic Magnolia Lane, the road leading to the clubhouse of Augusta National, the thick clouds, as if on cue, parted. I could see blue skies and rays of sunshine.

And if that wasn't enough, upon arrival at the clubhouse I was informed that we would be playing the course with the Masters' traditional Sunday pin placements. It was less than two weeks after the tournament, and the green and white scoreboards and many of the grandstands were still erect. The stage for my grand finale couldn't have been more perfect. I couldn't have been happier.

Eighteen glorious holes later—when I'd finally finished the round—I didn't know whether to dance a jig or cry. My quest was over and my dream fulfilled. For eight years I'd walked, ridden, and even crawled the finest golf courses of the world, having the time of my life.

And along the way I pocketed a lifetime of memories. Turn the page and let me tell you about them.

1

The Roots

Because I was born and raised in Palo Alto, California, you'd think that golf naturally became a part of my life. After all, Stanford University had a nearby course, and the Olympic Club and San Francisco Golf Club were only a short drive away. A mere two hours or so south were Pebble Beach Golf Links, Cypress Point Club and Spyglass Hill Golf Course.

Yet, like many teens growing up in the early 1950s, I didn't have golf on my radar. At the time, my goals were to play as much basketball and football as I could while working small jobs to bring home at least some form of spending money. The last thing I ever thought about was going out to play golf, although my mother and father, two blue-collar workers, seemed to enjoy the game and played as often as they could.

My mother, Mariette, and my father, Leon C.

Wentz, played at the local municipal golf course whenever they had the chance or some extra money. They were extremely fond of the game. I remember each Christmas they would always receive something related to golf as gifts, and this was before golf hats, windbreakers, and golf shirts were even available. "Wow, some loose balls and a box of tees," I would snicker to myself.

Later, as a young adult in college, I would often make Sunday visits to my parents. As soon as I opened the door, they would tell me to be quiet because someone on television was putting, hitting a drive, or whatever. I always had to wait for the commercials before I could say something.

During those years, I got my dose of golf, although it was still not a favorite activity. I tried to get into it—even went as far as playing—but golf just didn't click for me. I was left-handed, and at that time left-handed golfers were as rare as a hole-in-one on a par four.

Attending UCLA at the time, I thought of golf as something for mom and dad to enjoy. I wasn't interested. For me, sports meant football, rugby, and wrestling, although I did have four fraternity brothers who made up one-half of the UCLA men's golf team. At the time, the members of the golf team had this ritual of following dinner by lining up in front of the large living-room glass door to see the reflections of their swings. Thanks to mom and dad, I knew what they were trying to do, yet I still didn't get it.

Following my graduation, I spent a few years in

the military, but soon had the inkling to settle down. It was the late 1950s when getting married was the thing to do, and I felt ready.

I married my sweetheart, Jeanie Townley, and soon had three children—Brad, Craig, and Julie. As for work, I started my own construction company at the age of 23. Still, I played no golf and wouldn't for quite some time.

But, almost exactly 23 years after I formed my construction company, golf somehow again became a part of my life. The spark was the annual Crosby Pebble Beach National Pro-Am held at nearby Pebble Beach Golf Links.

Founded by world-famous crooner Bing Crosby, the tournament was something both my wife and I found fascinating, not just for the golf but for the entertainment value. Where else could you watch celebrities like Crosby, Bob Hope, Phil Harris, Dean Martin, and other stars tee it up?

In addition, the Goodyear blimp took gorgeous shots that highlighted the landscape and ocean, which even today define golf at Pebble Beach.

It was during one of those broadcasts one afternoon that I—now in my mid 40s—stretched from my reclining chair and turned to my wife and said, "You know, I've never even been to Pebble Beach and it's less than 100 miles away. It's so beautiful and I think we need and deserve a second home."

"That sounds great to me, but you don't even play golf."

"Yeah, I know I don't."

Nevertheless, a little less than two weeks later,

Jeanie and I were in Pebble Beach searching for a home site. Within a month, we were fortunate enough to purchase a site on the 15th fairway at Pebble Beach backing up to the fairway of No.4. An architect was soon called in, and two years later we had our second home. Thankfully, those last 20-plus years of working so hard had paid off.

Upon completion of the house, my friends and colleagues soon began hammering me. "Leon, you dummy, you built a home at Pebble Beach and you don't even play the game." My reply, which became custom, was, "It's a great investment." I still had no urge to play, but things were changing. Maybe it was the memories of my mother and father or the fact that I indeed now owned a home at of all places Pebble Beach—I was getting the itch.

Within the year, I was discussing my situation with a friend and he asked me if I would be interested in joining Menlo Country Club, a local golf club near our primary home in Atherton, California. Golf was coming to me, or was it the golf deep inside me coming out? This time, I said yes and within a few years, I was a member of the club.

While it took 47 years, I had finally been bitten by the golf bug, and after my first few rounds all I could think about was why I had waited so darn long. I instantly became hooked, and like any other golfer wanted to improve as fast as I could. Yet, rather than taking lessons, I simply started playing as much as my schedule allowed. I felt, having been an athlete, that I would eventually figure it all out. Sure enough, not taking lessons would haunt me early on. As I quickly found out, there's a reason why even players like Jack Nicklaus and Tiger Woods sometimes struggle. It's golf. No one has ever truly mastered the game and no one ever will.

For years, I fought an uphill battle to master the game, regardless of countless hours reading 30 how-to books and watching instructional videos. Being left-handed slightly compounded my woes. Everything that I read or watched had to be turned backwards. When the book said right hip, I thought left hip. Left shoulder was right shoulder and so on and so on. Stubbornly, I still put off taking actual lessons from a pro, thinking that I could still solve what I now know is one of sport's greatest puzzles—the golf swing. Not taking lessons is one of the regrets of my early golfing life.

One Man's Opinion
Best Three-Hole Stretch
Nos. 8, 9 and 10, Pebble Beach
Cliffs of doom
Best Starting Hole
No.1, Spyglass Hill
600-yard, par-five into the wind
Best Finishing Hole
No.18, Pebble Beach
Beauty and the beast
Best Caddies
Pebble Beach
Know the course and great storytellers

Nevertheless, the itch was growing stronger. Because I had my new home in Pebble Beach, it was natural that I should take my swings at Pebble Beach Golf Links.

While my quest to play the world's Top 100 golf courses was not yet official, Pebble Beach Golf Links, which opened in 1919, has always been regarded as one of the world's greatest golfing venues. The green fees were $125 at the time, but I felt that if tourists were playing there, I should be out there.

Finally, one afternoon, I packed my golf bag and off I went, getting in my first round at one of the world's greatest courses. Suffice to say, this rookie wasn't ready for the grand lady, as my scorecard easily testified. After my first round, I kept coming back to the course and every time left humbled.

Looking for what I thought would be a break, I later decided I would shift my attack to Pebble Beach Golf Links' sister course, Spyglass Hill Golf Course, which was designed by Robert Trent Jones Sr. and opened in 1966. Alas, I quickly found myself facing yet a larger monster.

Today, one of the three courses used during the annual AT&T Pebble Beach National Pro-Am, Spyglass Hill features different scenery, has a few more deer bolting here and there, and is less expensive than Pebble Beach Golf Links. Thing was, I soon discovered that the course has a higher slope rating and degree of difficulty than Pebble Beach Golf Links.

Again, my scorecard would suffer, yet by now the golf bug had consumed me.

Little did I know at the time that those early days at Pebble Beach Golf Links and Spyglass Hill—while at times brutal—would become the primary stepping stones on what would eventually become my quest.

2

Interest Keeps Growing

Suddenly a veteran of both Pebble Beach and Spyglass Hill, I began to expand my horizons. Like many new players, I started subscribing to various golf magazines and became a member of both the United States Golf Association and the Northern California Golf Association.

I began watching more golf tournaments, either on television or in person, hoping to later copy the players' mannerisms and style of play. While I struggled with the fact that I was left-handed, one of my favorite players to watch was Jack Nicklaus. I had immersed myself in a number of Nicklaus's instructional books and found that whenever he played, he always followed his own swing credo to the tee. What Jack wrote, he did. What he wrote, I followed in practice and when playing. It was my first lesson in the goal of being consistent. Along with teaching me to stick to a routine, the Nicklaus books also taught me to always think before playing a shot. To this day, I remember a section that basically stated, "If your line is blocked by a tree, and you are a 12-handicap or higher, always aim for the tree because chances are you will miss it, whereas on the other hand, if you are lower than 12-handicap, aim to miss the tree because odds are you will miss it." Suffice to say, I've saved some trees over the years by aiming at them.

My quest to play the world's Top 100 golf courses was still not officially under way, yet I was soon able to check another course off the list.

In the summer of 1987, the U.S. Open championship arrived at the nearby Olympic Club (Lake Course) in San Francisco. A year before the event, I had noticed that various types of business sponsorships were being solicited for the event and that some packages included not only tickets, programs and sponsor recognition, but also a group instruction hosted by Jack Nicklaus himself and two free rounds on Olympic Club's Lake Course.

Business savvy and now golf hungry, I didn't take very long to make the decision to become a sponsor. After all, I couldn't pass up a chance to watch Jack Nicklaus teach live, and I was guaranteed the opportunity to play the majestic Olympic Club Lake Course under U.S. Open conditions.

Slated to host the U.S. Open again in 2012, after having last hosted the championship in 1998, the Olympic Club was and is today a true test. Under USGA conditions, the course was even tougher. Already narrow and tree-lined, the course was tighter than a Gordian knot. Rough up to my ankles and greens quicker than lightning made a long playing day for me, yet unbeknownst to me at the time I again had notched another course on the list.

As for the Nicklaus clinic, I was again thrilled. This time, however, I looked to pass on the golf bug, as my parents did in my youth. Thanks to my sponsorship, I received two tickets to the Nicklaus clinic, which included the opportunity to watch the "Golden Bear" play the first nine holes at the Lake Course. Knowing that my kids were also avid Nicklaus fans, I gave the tickets for the clinic to my sons, Brad and Craig, both in their early 20s at the time. While I would have liked to watch, I'll never regret my decision. Upon the boys' arrival at home that evening, they couldn't stop talking. They were so excited!

Turned out, Nicklaus had picked my younger son Craig out of the crowd and used him as a model during the clinic. The Golden Bear invited my son into his den.

It wasn't long after that memorable U.S. Open in 1987 that things would again turn. Not long after the USGA and champion Scott Simpson left the Olympic Club, I was contacted by an old friend of mine named Doug Adams. Apparently Doug had attended college at UC Berkeley with then-current Cypress Point Club head pro Jim Langley and had the privilege of occasionally being able to play Cypress Point. Knowing that I was quickly becoming a major golf nut, Doug invited Brad, Craig, and me to join him as guests one day on the prestigious course. Of course, it was a no-brainer. I immediately accepted the invitation and notified my sons.

Designed by Dr. Alister MacKenzie, Cypress Point Club has been described as the meeting place of golf and heaven. On the front-nine, players experience hole-by-hole a golf course within itself. Not one hole is like any other hole. One hole you're battling the sand dunes, the next hole you're fighting uphill. If the Cypress Point front-nine holes were a puzzle, you'd think the pieces would not fit together. Yet they do, with magnificence being the cornerstone.

As for the back-nine, one always first starts thinking about the ocean holes—No.15, No.16 and No.17. On this glorious day, my first trip around the course with my sons, we finished up the par-four 14th and began heading across world-famous 17-Mile Drive to play the ocean holes. Then we met a local sheriff standing in our way guarding the path to the tee at No.15. Apparently, a few days earlier a group of tourists who weren't aware that they were on the grounds of Cypress Point Club had parked their cars and walked onto the course to get a closer look at the scenery. Even more amazingly, they had set up a mini barbecue with beer and all the trimmings in the middle of the 15th green and had their radio blaring. All the while their kids played with toys in the bunkers. The sheriff had arrived and explained that they were trespassing on private property. The group replied that they had paid their entrance fee to enter the 17-Mile Drive, and thus they should be allowed to picnic anywhere they pleased. The sher-

iff told them that they would be arrested. The threat
of arrest was something the group did understand.
They packed their belongings and left. The sheriff
gave us the go-ahead, and we went on to play some
of the most breathtaking holes in all of golf including No.16, which features a tee shot over a chasm of
churning sea.

During the spring of 1988, not long after our
round at Cypress Point, my elder son Brad told me
that he had fallen in love with
a beautiful young woman
named Darci and planned to
marry her. Darci, who grew
up in Arizona, had recently
moved to the Bay Area where
she and Brad met. I knew
Brad wanted to propose and I
wondered how he planned to
do it.

As usual, Brad tapped into
his creativity. Knowing we
had a second home in Pebble

> ## One Man's Opinion
>
> Most Scenic Course
> Cypress Point
> *One of a kind*
>
> Best Water Hole
> No.16, Cypress Point
> *224-yard par-three into
> the wind*
>
> Best Drink
> Sam's Special,
> Cypress Point
> *Fantastic*

Beach, he came up with the idea to propose to Darci
on the glorious green at No.7 at Pebble Beach Golf
Links. Arguably the most-photographed golf hole in
the world, No.7 at Pebble Beach Golf Links is like an
island in the middle of Carmel Bay. While short in
length, it's protected by rocks, numerous bunkers,
and the wind. During the 1992 U.S. Open, champion Tom Kite one day played the hole with a sand
wedge. The next day, he used a 6-iron.

Brad planned the event, setting a time of around

6 p.m. to pop the question, with the knowledge that it was about that time that the last group of the day would finish up at No.7. He had the Beach Club set up and cater a dinner on the green, complete with a white tablecloth, sterling silver and candles. The old tee box at No.8 would be the food prep area.

Darci, unbeknownst to her, would be picked up at her girlfriend's house—all of her friends knew what was up—in the Bay Area by a limousine and driven to No.7 where Brad and crew were waiting. They would be served champagne, a Caesar salad, grilled salmon, and finally a chocolate truffle dessert, which upon arrival, was to mark the time for Brad to propose.

Early on, everything went exactly as planned. Darci arrived not knowing a thing. There was zero wind. The preparations and the food were fantastic. Just as Brad was set to drop to his knee, however, the irrigation sprinklers began pumping away! Everyone packed up and ran for drier ground.

Indeed, no matter what preparation you make, things don't always go the way you want them to. Yet, in a way that's life. Even when things go horribly wrong there's still a beauty to it. As for Brad and Darci, the proposal took an unexpected turn, but they've gone on to be happily married and have since provided me even more joy by giving me three terrific grandchildren—Taylor, Zack, and Ryan.

As for me, not long after Darci and Brad married in 1989, Jeanie, my wife of 30 years, fell ill with pancreatic cancer. A mere three months after her initial diagnosis, she would pass away at the age of 50. Jeanie and I had first started dating back in the early

1950s as high school sweethearts. Devastated, I turned to golf as my outlet.

For more than a year, I played as a single as much as I could. The time on a golf course gave me time to reflect and time to rearrange my life. Having lost my wife, I made golf my best friend.

About a year and a half following Jeanie's passing, however, my life took another turn, and then it once again became a straightaway. While still recovering from my loss, I met a lovely woman named Cathy Salmon who had been friends with Jeanie. Love was lost, but love was gained. I soon remarried. Life, as it always does, was again moving forward.

Not very long after marrying Cathy I discovered that one of her dearest friends was married to a member of the Colonial Country Club in Fort Worth, Texas. Host of the 1941 U.S. Open, Colonial Country Club has a rich history with a membership that once included legend Ben Hogan. To this day, the course still hosts the Bank of America Colonial championship, a regular stop on the PGA Tour.

As at Cypress Point Club, I would need some help in getting to play. At Colonial's my host-member was Gray Mills, a former football star at Texas Christian University. Gray provided me with my first exposure to a golf course outside of California, and he and I quickly became close friends. Later, Cathy and I would have Gray and his wife Nelda as our guests at both the AT&T Pebble Beach National Pro-Am and the 2000 U.S. Open.

As Cathy and I began our lives together, we soon started discussing various vacation spots where we both could play some golf. Earlier in her life, Cathy lived for a time in Edinburgh, Scotland, and while she thought the cuisine was forgettable, she did remind me that Scotland was the birthplace of golf. As we began preparing for our overseas trip, I started chatting with everyone I knew who had been to Scotland, especially those who had played golf there.

Then, one day I was reading a golf journal and found an article that mentioned the availability of golf travel agencies that could help one plan a golf vacation. I gave Adventures in Golf a call asking for details and costs. The agency also gave me references to past customers who lived in my area. I called those references and heard nothing but praise. "Leon, you have to go! Scotland is a great experience. The golf is a bit different than here and you should pack some rain gear, but by all means go!"

Weeks later, Cathy and I confirmed our plans and were on our way. It would be the first leg of what would eventually become my quest.

CHAPTER

3

A Wee Bit of Scotland

In the spring of 1993, Cathy and I arrived in Scotland. For me, it was a completely new world. For Cathy, it was somewhat of a homecoming. Like most American golfers who are making their first golfing trip to Scotland, we wanted to taste the history. Among the courses on our list were Gleneagles, The Links at St. Andrews, Cruden Bay, Royal Dornoch, and Muirfield.

Using her familiarity with the countryside, Cathy played the role of travel guide with the help of Adventures in Golf's principal Ken Hamill, who booked our trip. Upon landing in Glasgow, in southwest Scotland, Cathy and I rented a car and proceeded to drive northeast for a few hours to Auchterarder, home of the Gleneagles Golf Resort. Because it was springtime, the drive was gorgeous. Vivid green grass and bright yellow daffodils crowded the roadsides.

Amid the hills a large magnificent mansion came into view. It was the Gleneagles Hotel, regarded as one of the finest hotels in the world. Adjacent to the hotel were not one, not two, but *three* inland courses: the King's Course, the Queen's Course and the PGA Centenary Course, a newer course that had been designed by my hero, Jack Nicklaus.

When it came time for me to tee off, I went with tradition and played the King's Course, which features stunning views of the Trossachs and Ben Vorlich peaks. I was thrilled to be playing my first inland Scottish course, yet my scorecard again somewhat suffered. Following my round, I remember my caddie Ian stating, "You had a bit of a poor score today, didn't you, Leon?" All I could answer was, "Yes, I did at that."

When playing a course for the first time, I generally make it a practice to hire a caddie to help me navigate the course. That's the caddie's job, to be your guide. Ian, an older gentleman, had been a caddie at Gleneagles for over 50 years. He was extremely experienced and knew the course like the back of his hand. Unfortunately, my game that day didn't complement his fine work.

Yet it wasn't just my game that was aching. Weeks before we left for our trip, an old bone spur on my right heel had flared up. It had become such a nuisance that just before our trip I decided to visit my physician to have it checked out. He said, "Leon, it's very inflamed and you should rest and stay off it as much as you possibly can." "But, doctor," I replied, "I'm leaving in days for a golf trip to Scotland that

I've been planning for a long time and only one course that I know of has carts. Walking will be a must." As I walked off the course with Ian that first day on the links, my doctor's advice echoed in my mind. I was indeed in more pain than I had been at home. I shrugged it off—there was golf to be played.

A day after our experience at Gleneagles, Cathy and I were again on the road, this time headed towards the town of St. Andrews, home to the birth-place of golf, St. Andrews Links. At that time, getting onto the course was extremely difficult because of demand. The course is owned by the city of St. Andrews, whose policy dictates that half of all tee-times be set aside for local citizens, with tourists, certain local golf clubs and other nonresidents getting the other half through a lottery system.

One Man's Opinion
Most Traditional Course
St. Andrews
The birthplace of golf
Best Links Course
Muirfield
The epitome of true Scottish golf
Best Lodging
Greywalls Hotel, Muirfield
Makes you want to forget about playing

From what I had learned, the wait is usually not long but could extend to a few days. Luckily for us, we gained a preset time by joining a colleague who happened to be a member of an outside club located in St. Andrews.

All set to go off, I was greeted by one of St. Andrews' veteran caddies, Jon. Jon was at one time a champion golfer. He knew the course inside and out and, more importantly, he radiated Scottish charm. If I had ever envisioned a caddie at St. Andrews, Jon was the guy. A lot of his habits reminded me of the book "A Wee Nip at the 19th Hole," which was written by a caddie master at St. Andrews and tells the story of the evolution of the caddie in Scotland.

As I stepped to the first tee, I admit I was consumed by the moment. Surrounded by golf history, I was about to hit my first shot in the birthplace of golf. On my right was the historic starter shack, while on my left was the green at No.18. Directly behind me loomed the glorious Royal and Ancient Golf Club building. As if that wasn't enough, a small gallery of visitors stood near the first tee watching each player tee off. Absolutely, by no means, was a player allowed a mulligan or second try. Upon my turn, I got the ball out there. I would have liked to have had a mulligan, but I was off. I had played links-style courses before, but this would be the first time I had ever played a Scottish-style links course.

The course layout was very simple. The front-nine went straight to the coastline where you turned around—a full 180 degrees—and headed straight back. Among the differences I noticed between St. Andrews and other links courses I had played was that St. Andrews' fairways were very natural-looking and nonirrigated, as if they always belonged there. Also, the greens were at times enormous, up to 6,000 square feet, hard and anything but flat. As for the rough, stray too far and you ended up in natural gorse at a height of 12 to 18 inches. There were also the pothole bunkers. Invisible most of the time, a pothole bunker at St. Andrews can swallow you up and spit you out. The bunkers can be so nasty they all have names, the most infamous being Hell on No.14. Land in Hell, and you're almost guaranteed to lose a stroke.

A true links course sits on the land situated between the ocean and where workable farmland usually begins in a flat and sometimes lightly mounded area that requires no improvement except for tee boxes and greens that are man-made. The fairways are natural and more often than not nonirrigated. The fairways are reasonably wide, maybe 30 or so yards across and the rough can vary. The rough, usually heavily grown gorse that ranges from three to 18 inches, seldom yields a clean club-head path to one's ball. A good caddie with keen eyesight is the key, and often caddies locate balls by walking through the rough and feeling the ball with the soles of their feet.

While the weather for my day on the course was rather benign, I can't imagine someone playing the Old Course through rain and high winds. It would be like trying to traverse a minefield. Then again, there's that other Scottish tradition to look forward to, that being a wee nip of single malt at the 19th hole.

Overall, getting the chance to play St. Andrews was a thrill and a moment I'll never forget. Following No.17, I walked with Jon across the famous Swilcan Bridge, which was originally built by the Romans to cross Swilcan Burn. In Scotland, a burn is a small meandering creek with water. Thing is, if your ball lands in a burn, it's then called a ditch. In recent years, the bridge has become the site where retiring golf legends—Arnold Palmer, Jack Nicklaus—pause to celebrate their past accomplishments on the Old Course. While not even close to the legends, even I felt a chill crossing the Swilcan Bridge. You can't escape the history. Walking up the 18th fairway, I felt like I had won the British Open. However, another concern pressed on my mind— the increasing discomfort caused by my bone spur.

A day after play at St. Andrews, Cathy and I headed up the eastern coastline of Scotland to Cruden Bay Golf Club just north of Aberdeen. Cruden Bay, like St. Andrews, seemed to have been there forever. It was originally commissioned by the Great North of Scotland Railway Company in 1894, yet legend has it that golf was being played there as early as 1791. It would not surprise me. The course, while at times a bit strange in design, like St. Andrews, is as natural as they get. This time, I had the pleasure of playing with three older Scotsmen who were very helpful in showing me where to go and what to watch out for. During my round, my heel indeed flared up again, so much that I was barely able to finish.

After putting out on No.18, Cathy met us and she and the older gentlemen had to physically assist me to the clubhouse, where I was treated to potato soup for lunch. Having seen me in such agony, the Scotsmen referred me to a local physician where I could pick up some pain reliever. I told them all about our trip, and mentioned that our itinerary still included golf at Royal Dornoch Golf Club and Muirfield Golf Club. We also planned to extend our trip for a week in Rome, which is regarded as a walking city.

After a visit with the good doctor, Cathy and I headed still farther north to play Royal Dornoch, which was designed by golf legend Old Tom Morris. Back in the late 1890s, Morris was golf's Nicklaus. Along the way, when we stopped for lunch, Cathy saw that I was still unable to put any weight on my heel. She asked if we should cut the trip short and head home. It didn't take me a split second to reply, "No way. Somehow, I have to play the remaining two courses because I may never be here again." We started thinking about getting some crutches, but could one even play on crutches? If so, where would we even find crutches? Oddly enough, as we continued our drive and our discussion, Cathy noticed a young woman on crutches. We stopped and asked her where we could obtain a pair. "Just go to Dr. Gray's Hospital," the woman replied, as if we were locals. After explaining that we were tourists, we got some directions and were on our way.

Upon arriving at Dr. Gray's Hospital in Elgin, we went straight to the emergency room and asked how we might be able to obtain some crutches—buy, rent, whatever. After a few brief minutes, an orderly returned with a pair, stating, "Here, you can take this old wooden pair if they fit." We asked about compensation, to which the orderly replied, "There is no cost. When you are finished using them just deliver them to the closest Post Office. They'll return them here free of charge."

As we left Dr. Gray's, Cathy and I chuckled. We couldn't believe how easy it was to get the crutches. Back home, we would have spent the entire day filling out paperwork. We were back on the road north to Inverness and Dornoch within 30 minutes.

When we arrived at Royal Dornoch, we got our

first taste of true Scottish weather. It was very cold and windy. Apparently, a day before there had been a sleet storm. As I hobbled my way into the pro shop, I was asked if I needed any assistance. I told the man, "I have a tee-time, have requested a caddie and I'm ready to go." The expressions on the staff's faces were of bewilderment. They thought I was absolutely loony.

After they realized I wasn't kidding, they assigned a caddie to us and with Cathy and the caddie in tow I went forward to the first tee. I had no idea how the crutches would work and really didn't care too much about my scoring potential. Looking back, I'm glad I didn't care about my score because the crutches obviously made things interesting. Then again, I did make par on the 410-yard uphill 17th hole. Considering the circumstances, it remains one of the greatest pars in my life and it didn't go unrecognized. After I finished at No.18, an older gentleman came running out of the club bar yelling, "I heard you soldiered No.17, you soldiered No.17, did you not?" I replied, "Well, yes I did." With that, the gentleman ushered Cathy and me directly to the clubhouse where we were treated to lunch. This is what made my quest so memorable, and why I still play golf today—the people.

With Royal Dornoch checked off my list, I felt a little more confident that I would be able to finish my golf trip. After all, I only had one more course to play, that one being Muirfield. Question was, how would the folks at stuffy old Muirfield react to a guy on crutches? I would soon find out.

Following our visit to Dornoch, Cathy and I drove south for about five hours to the charming small town of Gullane, the home of Muirfield. Muirfield, like St. Andrews, is one of Scotland's oldest and most traditional links courses. Since 1892, it has hosted 14 British Opens. Muirfield is also home to The Honourable Company of Edinburgh Golfers, a golf club whose roots go back to 1744.

Arriving the day before my scheduled round, I thought I should pay a visit to the caddie master, tell him my situation, and find out whether or not the club would even allow me to play. During my brief visit, the caddie master listened very closely to my tale and told me he'd have an answer sometime before my slated tee time, which was 10 a.m. the following day. That sounded fine with me. What was I supposed to expect, anyway? Afterwards, I hobbled off to meet Cathy at our hotel—the Greywalls Hotel—which sat adjacent to Muirfield.

I was by now somewhat anxious regarding my plight, but Greywalls put me at ease. Along with being a simply charming boutique hotel, Greywalls allows guests among other things the privileges to make one's own drink and sign in for a cigar. All amid an environment that defines the beauty of life in Scotland. I myself found great pleasure in sitting with Cathy in front of a small fireplace just relaxing and resting my sore heel.

After what turned out to be a rejuvenating evening, I awoke feeling a little bit nervous. It was time to revisit the caddie master and discover my fate. Upon meeting him he stated, "Yes, you can attempt to play. This is your caddie, this is your buggy cart, and these are the special rules and conditions."

All it took for me was to hear the word "Yes." I was relieved, yet there was more to it than that. Instead of a regular golf cart, the buggy was some kind of tiny old tractor-type rig used to cut the nearby fields. The caddie master went on. "In regard to the buggy, the caddie will be the only driver. You may ride on the modified jump seat. Just hang your crutches and golf bag wherever you can. When you get to the greens, it is important that you do not use the crutches on them. We've had very heavy rains and the crutches will damage the greens. With that, good luck and play well."

At our precise tee-time, the caddie, our buggy and I were off to start what would be one of the strangest rounds of my life. Things began with the buggy. Unfamiliar with the old machine, the caddie early on had trouble maneuvering the thing. It was hopping all over the place like it had a mind of its own, truly dieseling. Fortunately, at the time there weren't many players on the course. Those who were, however, were definitely baffled. They had a look like, "Who are these guys, and what the hell are they doing?" On the home course of the Honourable Company of Edinburgh Golfers, my caddie and I drove around in a jalopy. Mr. Wentz and his fantastic flying machine.

On the course, the fairways and rough weren't too hard to navigate but when we got to a green, things became interesting. At each green we'd dismount the buggy and approach it with the caddie carrying my bag and me hobbling on my crutches.

As we got on the green, I dropped my crutches and proceeded to crawl to my ball. I would then stand up, the caddie would hand me my putter and I would attempt to putt out. After finishing the hole, I would crawl back off the green, get my crutches from my caddie and hobble back to the buggy for our next hole. As for just how large some of the greens can be on a links course, I'll say this: The grass stains from my day at Muirfield never did come out.

Eventually, my caddie, our buggy and I finished the round to the applause of the caddie master. Upon putting out on No.18, the caddie master was right there to shake my hand and congratulate me on playing my first round at Muirfield. I would imagine it's still one of the weirdest rounds ever played at the course. Yet, I did it.

Afterwards, I headed back to the comfort of Greywalls looking like I had not played golf but rugby instead. Cathy was there waiting, and we enjoyed another restful time with snacks before a cozy fireplace.

Our Scotland trip was completed. It was time to look forward to the second half of our vacation, a trip to Rome. We again discussed whether or not we should cut it short and return home. Again, I said that we were on perhaps a once-in-a-lifetime trip. The crutches be damned! Suffice to say, we made it to Rome, where we enjoyed the sights of the Spanish Steps, the Vatican and the Coliseum, all with me on crutches.

Days later, we were back home in the Bay Area, setting up plans for our next vacation.

CHAPTER

4

Green, Green Greens

In 1994, I still had not officially kicked off my quest. Slowly but surely, though, I was starting to check some courses off the list. After all, courses like Pebble Beach, Cypress Point, and St. Andrews have been and always will be regarded as some of the finest venues in the world. As for our next planned excursion, Cathy and I thought about how much we had enjoyed Scotland. By the fall, we had set up our next vacation. This time, we would head to Ireland.

Our friends and colleagues always spoke highly of the beauty and the great people of Ireland. Of course, there was also terrific golf. During our planning, I realized there are three significant parts to every vacation: anticipation, making the trip, and returning home with memories whether from photographs or new friends we made. Other factors are the time of year and potential weather. A great example in the U.S. is Minnesota. Go there in the summer and you're swamped by mosquitoes and the humidity. In the winter, meanwhile, you can't find enough parkas to wear.

The timing of our trip to Ireland mattered less since we'd likely encounter wind and rain, which falls there 150 to 225 days per year. Consulting again with our travel agent, we decided on a fairly simple trip. We'd fly from San Francisco to London, then on to Belfast where we would proceed to visit among other courses Royal Portrush, Royal County Down, Portmarnock, Lahinch, and Ballybunion.

After an extremely turbulent flight, we landed in Belfast and proceeded to head straight for Royal Portrush Golf Club. Opened in 1888, Royal Portrush in 1895 hosted the first-ever professional golf tournament held in Ireland. It was redesigned by Harry S. Colt in 1929. For decades it has hosted the Irish Amateur and in 1951, it hosted the British Open.

The course has a lot of tricky greens but with the help of knowledgeable caddies we mastered them, even the one on its most famous and dangerous No.14, Calamity. Even my heel cooperated—no pain. It was a great way to start our second trip across the pond.

Afterwards, we followed our round at Royal Portrush with a quick lunch. We then hopped in our rental car and headed south to Newcastle, home of Royal County Down Country Club. Early the next morning, it was time to take on Royal County Down, another legendary Irish layout that Tom Watson once described as "the purest links course in the world." Little did I know, but something special was indeed waiting at Royal County Down, the host site of the 2007 Walker Cup.

Arriving at the first tee at Royal County Down, I was greeted by a caddie known as "One Ball." I quickly found out how he had earned his nickname. After teeing off, we played rather quickly, always using, well, one ball. As is the norm in Scotland and Ireland, a foursome is expected to be finished with their rounds in three to three-and-a-half hours. No mulligans. Don't even think about it. Move along. Hit when ready.

While in the fairway of No.3, however, I looked over at the green on No.4 and noticed a fellow who looked and walked exactly like a friend of mine back home. Becoming more quizzical, I walked towards him and began shouting,

"John? John, is that you?"

"Leon? Is that you?" came the reply.

Lo and behold, it was a friend of mine named John Griffiths, an attorney whom I knew from the States. More amazingly, I knew the entire foursome!

Later on No.10, "One Ball" and I caught up with John and his group. After a quick exchange of hand-shakes, smiles and pleasantries, they let us play through. In my glee, I promised them that when we were all finished with our rounds, lunch at the 19th hole would be on me.

A few holes later, I asked "One Ball" if there might be any other foursomes ahead of us. At the time he wasn't sure and we played on. But on the tee box at No.12, we did catch another foursome.

Once again we exchanged pleasantries when a fellow said, "Leon Wentz? Leon, is that you?"

I hesitated then replied, "Ken? Ken Winton? You have to be kidding me!"

I was stunned because I also knew the players in the other foursome. I mentioned to Ken my agreement with John, and we all went along shaking our heads in amazement. Indeed, it is a small world after all. At the time, only nine players were on this world-class course, all coming from a place—the Bay Area—that was 6,000 miles away. More amazingly, we all lived within four miles of one another.

To this day, when we see one another we marvel at that fateful day. It still seems so impossible, yet it happened. That's the power of the game of golf. Whether or not you're a beginner, an amateur, or a professional, you're part of a fraternity. You're a golfer, and golf is an international language that every player understands.

Then again, there's still national pride. After our remarkable day at Royal County Down in Northern Ireland, Cathy and I the next morning arrived at Portmarnock Golf Club in the Republic of Ireland, the site of multiple Irish Opens and the 1991 Walker Cup. While checking in at Portmarnock, we felt some strange vibes from the staff. The source, we learned, was that a day earlier one of their longtime members was key in Europe's defeat of the Americans in the annual Ryder Cup championship. Because we were Americans, we heard the story more than once.

Don't think for a second that the Ryder Cup

doesn't mean anything. It means a lot, especially to the Europeans. While a bit uncomfortable for understandable reasons, we still got in our round. One of my lasting impressions of Portmarnock was the course's final five holes. They were a great way to finish what was a rather strange day.

A day after our experience at Portmarnock, we took a short drive to unranked County Louth Golf Club, which in 2004, hosted the Irish Open. The day we played County Louth, the course looked a bit haggard and the winds were up. Nevertheless, it was the day I carded my first-ever eagle.

At the time, the par-four, 332-yard 14th hole was playing downwind. I hit an average drive that carried with the wind down the left-hand side of the fairway. Arriving at my second shot, I was a mere 90 yards from the green. I used a low 8-iron approach to hit the ball, which after landing danced its way into the heart of the green. I knew it was a nice shot, but little did I know how great it was. Reaching the green, my caddie and I began a hunt to find my ball. We all agreed that it looked like a nice shot, but we couldn't locate the ball. Finally, my caddie checked the one place where I would never have looked. There it was in the cup! My first-ever eagle had landed!

Riding a wave of elation, Cathy and I the following day looked to peak again at our next scheduled stop, Lahinch Golf Club on the west coast of Ireland. When we got to Lahinch, another Old Tom Morris creation nestled among dunes bordering the sea like Cypress Point Club, we were greeted by a severe storm that for the last few days had been churning off the Atlantic coast. On the way to Lahinch, I had thoughtfully purchased five gloves in case of bad weather. Good thing that I bought so many. I used them all until they were ragged and soaked through.

On the course, the wind was whipping and the rain came in buckets. Interestingly enough, early on the wind helped cure my slice. Later, when we got to the back-nine the sun broke through. It was at that point that I fully understood why Ireland is regarded as the land of the green. Under

> **One Man's Opinion**
> Worst Weather #2
> Lahinch
> *Five golf gloves used, four inches of rain in four hours*

the sun and after a quick rain, it was like a green Wonderland.

Following our afternoon at Lahinch, Cathy and I headed south to play Ballybunion Golf Club, another of Ireland's most historic courses. Also situated on the west coast, Ballybunion is one of Tom Watson's favorites and throughout my round my caddie continuously chatted me up about the impact Watson—a five-time British Open champion—has recently had on the course and its members. At the time, renovation work was being done on a number of holes, all under the direction of Watson. Some members thought it was a terrific improvement, partly because he was their idol. Others said the course had never been altered, so why should they listen to Mr. Watson and his ideas? I left that one for the Irish to figure out, but

Ballybunion remains one of the world's truly great courses. When you have a course where land meets sea, it's almost a given that there is going to be magic.

The next day, Cathy and I wrapped up our Ireland trip by playing Killarney Golf Club, an unranked course. While unranked, Killarney had its charm. Overall, it was a modest but beautiful course that rests adjacent to Lake Killarney near the Ring of Fire in southwest Ireland. I was quickly finding out that there are scads of great courses out there. To make the Top 100 list, it has to be special.

When we finished our round, we headed back to our room where, upon turning on the television, we were met with the news that O.J. Simpson was just found not guilty. Indeed, it's a small world.

Flying back home to the Bay Area, we again reveled in what had been a wonderful golfing vacation. Scotland and Ireland were now checked off our list. Question was, where would we end up next, if anywhere? Would we plan another overseas getaway or stay close to home, maybe work on improving our games? Only time would tell.

5

The Open

The year after our trip to Ireland was somewhat quiet. While I still played an awful lot of golf, I, for the most part, remained at home. I had the urge to take another major golf vacation, but I knew that next time I would be going alone. After arriving home, Cathy had flown to the East Coast. During her flight, she experienced severe turbulence. So bad was her experience that Cathy, a former flight attendant for American Airlines, insisted afterwards that she would never fly again. With absolute love and understanding of her situation, I had to make some critical decisions. I still wanted to travel, more than ever. The golf bug had taken me over. Then again, Cathy had vowed to never fly again.

After a lengthy discussion we resolved this issue by agreeing that each of us should pursue personal goals of our fleeting lives with one another's full support. Ultimately, Cathy agreed that I should travel whenever I wanted by myself or with my kids. She would be with me not physically, but in heart.

Not long after we came to our conclusion, I was off again. Having been to Scotland and reading so much about the British Open, I decided that I would plan a return trip to watch the 126th Open at Royal Troon Golf Club. On the same trip, I would also play some of Britain's great courses that I had yet to set foot on. After doing some research, I found that the Open generally revolves around nine courses based in either England or Scotland: St. Andrews, Carnoustie, Turnberry, Troon, Muirfield, Royal Lytham, Royal Birkdale, Royal St. George's and Royal Liverpool, which just recently returned to rotation in the summer of 2006.

Previously, I had attended U.S. Opens at both Pebble Beach and the Olympic Club in San Francisco, while the only experience I had with the British Open was watching it on television. My plan was set. I would head across the Atlantic, meet some of my children who were already traveling in Europe, play golf, and attend the Open.

Yet a mere week after Cathy and I approved the go ahead, I was diagnosed with prostate cancer. It was of course a setback, but I moved on. Exploratory biopsies revealed that I needed surgery and I quickly agreed. I could only hope for good results and a rapid recovery, and that's what happened. Everything went fine during the surgery, and my recovery status was very positive. I would still make my trip despite some soreness.

In the summer of 1997, I flew from San

Francisco to Heathrow Airport in London. After landing I instantly began driving towards Dover and Royal St. George's Golf Club. In the States, the directions to a golf course are always right there on the road in front of you. Based on my previous trips overseas, I should have remembered that the directions in Britain can be somewhat daunting. In the case of Royal St. George's, very little signage pointed me the right way. Not until I drove through a field of horses and finally spotted a little, old-time clubhouse did I realize I was on the right track. At first glance, the course reminded me of my uncle's farm in South Dakota. There was hardly a tree in sight and the ground appeared relatively flat. Then again, there were the bunkers, one so huge it could house a Greyhound bus. The host of numerous Open championships, Royal St. George's may have looked benign but it was tough. It was and remains a true Open championship venue.

One Man's Opinion
Most Difficult Bunkers
Royal St. George's
The "Himalaya" bunker
Worst Starting Hole
No.1, Royal Lytham
206-yard, par-three

The following day, one which would turn out to be very busy, I headed north to play at Wentworth Golf Club (West Course), home to three championship courses. I played the original West Course, which first opened in 1926. The golf was great. Known locally as the Burma Road, the West Course winds its way through heavy woodland, making the fairways extremely tight. Both holes No.17 and No.18 are par fives. It was odd, but I liked it.

Unfortunately, I didn't have much time to reflect. I was in somewhat of a rush. Knowing my day was only half over, I finished my round, grabbed a quick bite, and immediately drove northeast on a five-hour trip that took me through Manchester on up to Southport where I was scheduled to play Formby Golf Club and Royal Lytham and St. Annes Golf Club. The bigger bonus, however, was that I was to be met by my daughter, my son, and my daughter-in-law, who had previously been touring Paris.

The next morning, the ladies headed for Liverpool to visit the Beatles Museum while Brad and I went to play Formby, a modest local private course. At the end of the day, we all hooked up again for what was an excellent English-style dinner at the clubhouse.

A good night's sleep later, we were all on the road north again, this time the destination being Royal Lytham and St. Annes Golf Club, just south of Blackpool. Founded in 1887, Royal Lytham has a rich history, having hosted numerous Ryder Cup championships and Open championships. The holes that stood out to me were No.1 and No.18. No.1 is a short par-three starter hole, which is extremely rare. During the 2001 Open, it was on this hole that Welshman Ian Woosnam was penalized two strokes for carrying too many clubs in his bag. At the time, Woosnam was three strokes off the lead. He never recovered and eventually fired his caddie for the error. No.18, meanwhile, was memorable because a year before my round, American Tom Lehman had walked up the 18th fairway with his father en route to claiming the claret jug. This time, it was my turn to walk up the 18th fairway with my son.

While we basked in our personal glory, we were, however, pressed for time. Following a quick lunch that included fish'n'chips and mushy peas with plenty of malt vinegar, we all jumped in the car for a five-hour drive to Glasgow, Scotland where we would next soak up two days of the Open championship at Royal Troon. As I have mentioned, I had attended U.S. Open championships before, but an Open championship is very different. Besides being played on a links course, the Open has greater attendance, legalized wagering, and a football game atmosphere.

The 1997 Open championship at Troon was Scotland's first chance to watch Tiger Woods play, and the fans responded in glee. The first day we were there, the attendance was estimated to be a record 65,000. The average crowd at a U.S. Open event is estimated to be around 25,000. The gallery was also much different from those in the U.S. At the Open, the crowd was a bit noisier, with a few more whistles sprinkling the air. Because Tiger Woods was making his first Open appearance, kids under the age of 12 were admitted free. The crowd was also more on the move. Under a bright blue and sunny sky many went shirtless and sunbathed, lying on the ground or as longtime Open commentator Peter Alliss described it, "taking an afternoon nap."

As for the championship, the leaderboard was constantly shuffling. On Sunday, as the tournament was coming to a close, we proceeded to the grandstands at No.18 to watch the final players come in. We were fortunate to have what could be described as "50-yard line" seats that gave us a splendid view of the action on the green and the famous yellow manually operated scoreboard and its large Rolex logo. We would later be treated to a surprise and spectacular finish as American Justin Leonard came out of nowhere to win the championship.

Afterwards, the closing ceremonies took place, which also held a surprise. Some things you just don't see on television. On this occasion, as Leonard was making his winner's speech, a young woman suddenly came bolting out of the crowd and onto the green wearing a trench coat. Soon, the coat was off, leaving her stark naked except for a tiger's tail and tiger's ears. It was obvious who she had been rooting for! It took about five minutes for officials and the police to corral her and whisk her away. Actually, it seemed as if they didn't know what to do with her once they did catch her. What a way to close what had been a terrific Open championship!

The next morning, we headed east to Gullane, Scotland for a return trip to Muirfield and the Greywalls Hotel, my favorite from our previous visit. On this day, my daughter and daughter-in-law played the No.4 course at Gullane Golf Club while my son and I played Muirfield. Later that evening we all celebrated my 60th birthday with a delicious dinner and a surprise birthday cake. It was a wonderful day, but alas it was time for us to part ways. By morning, the children were on a flight headed back to the States. Meanwhile, I drove my rental car to St. Andrews.

The Old Course was no stranger. I'd played it before but one never tires of playing a classic. When in Paris, one always wants to see the Eiffel Tower or visit Notre Dame. Doesn't matter how many times you've seen it before, you have to see it again. This time around, the tee-time process had changed, making it tougher to get on the Old Course. Thankfully, I wouldn't be affected since I was going to be playing as a guest of a friend of mine who lives in St. Andrews and is a member of one of the small private clubs that have been granted certain priorities. That day, I joined my friend and two of his buddies in a foursome. For them, it was their weekly round on the course. Imagine that, playing your weekly Saturday-morning round at St. Andrews! Nice deal.

They certainly knew the lay of the course and were very helpful for my second time playing the course. Nevertheless, I still found myself in a few blind pothole bunkers. My thrill came at holes No.17 and No.18, where I walked away with back-to-back pars. On No.17, a hole that Jack Nicklaus once described as "a par four and a half," my drive just carried over the corner of the Old Course Hotel, where it then bounced off a stone wall and caromed into the middle of the fairway. From there, I hit a fairway wood that found the green. I nearly made my birdie putt but got my par. I had made par on the infamous Road Hole! With another par at No.18, I walked away with a huge grin. I could only hope for such good fortune.

The next day, I was to play Carnoustie Golf Club. Carnoustie, which sits about 25 miles west of St.

Andrews, is renowned for eating up players and spitting them back out. In fact, some refer to the course as "Carnasty." It was at Carnoustie, two years after my visit, that Frenchman Jean Van de Velde would implode. In the 1999 Open championship, Van de Velde came to No.18, needing only to make a six to win the Open. He would go on to make seven in a moment that has since become infamous. On my day, the weather was relatively calm, but the course was still a brute. I, along with countless others, was a victim of Carnoustie.

Despite taking my lumps, I had little time to heal. That same day, I headed south past Glasgow to Turnberry, home of Turnberry Resort and Golf Club. A spectacular venue, Turnberry oozed Scotland. The hotel, which served as a hospital during World War II, stands on a hill that overlooks the Irish Sea, the island of Ailsa Craig and the three courses: Ailsa, Kintyre, and Arran. I played the Ailsa Course, which was the site of the famous 1977 British Open duel between Nicklaus and Watson. Again, should the wind blow, the course can be a brute. Luckily, on my day the wind was rather calm.

While the golf was great, one of the highlights for me at Turnberry was the evening tradition. Following a round, one can relax in the bar and enjoy a fine single malt whisky. As the sun begins to drop, bagpipes begin echoing through the air playing traditional Scottish music. Turnberry was Scotland in the palm of your hand.

Next, I drove 200 miles south to play Royal Birkdale Golf Club, which first opened in 1889. I found upon my arrival that the course at the time was undergoing major renovations in preparation for the 1998 British Open. Among the work being done was the removal of over 20,000 trees—a requirement of the Royal & Ancient, the governing body for the British Open—which was expected to make wind more of a factor. Being from California, I had to chuckle to myself. Such a thing would never be allowed to happen in the Golden State regardless of the reason because of the many environmental groups in the state. The course, while undergoing work, was still remarkable with its sand dunes. Walking away, I could see why the course was considered England's finest. The dunes reflect the shoreline location, making it another great test.

Next up was Royal Liverpool Golf Club. Royal Liverpool was a difficult course for me to locate in my little rental car. After a spell, I found it, a small modest brick clubhouse in Hoylake, a very blue-collar suburb of Liverpool. While watching the 2006 British Open on television, I did remember the buildings but not the course nor a single hole. In my opinion, the course has no signature holes. They are all tough and look alike with their brown, nonirrigated fairways. While watching the Open, I did notice there was very little wind compared to when I played the course. I played that venue in gale-force winds. The Irish Sea can create havoc at Royal Liverpool when it wants to.

What a year it was! Not only did I get to watch the British Open in person, but I got to play some of the event's most historic venues. Alas, it was time to head back home.

6

Making the Quest Official

T he winter of early 1998 was somewhat quiet. While I still played my local courses, for the most part, I stayed around home. It was during one evening at home, however, that another fuse ignited. The spark was a golf magazine article on a new Tom Weiskopf/Jay Moorish co-designed course—Loch Lomond Golf Club—which had just opened north of Glasgow, Scotland.

Might I become a member? After some research, I applied. Two overseas colleagues, already members, sponsored my application. Shortly thereafter in the spring of 1998, I was granted membership.

Within a few months I was again headed to Scotland with my son Brad accompanying me. At first glance, Loch Lomond Golf Club was indeed a magical site, as the critics had noted. Only four years after it opened in 1994, it quickly jumped into the Top 100 world rankings and was named one of

Europe's greatest tracks. South African Ernie Els, upon his first visit, called it the best in Europe.

Along with getting our first taste of Loch Lomond, Brad and I also got in rounds at Royal Troon Golf Club and Turnberry in Scotland. Then, the future site of the 2004 British Open, Royal Troon first opened in 1878. With my round there, I had now played every British Open venue. It was a very exciting trip, but also very short.

When I arrived home, I was confronted with stacks of unanswered correspondence and periodicals, including a new edition of *Golf Magazine's* Top 100 Courses in the World. Perusing the list numerous times, probably like a zillion others, I began mentally checking off the courses I had played.

Two courses that I noticed very quickly were Los Angeles Country Club and the San Francisco Golf Club. I had been a member at the Los Angeles Country Club for several years and continued to play it often, especially while on trips to UCLA. It is a very private club that is located on Wilshire Boulevard in the heart of Beverly Hills. The club has been approached several times by the USGA requesting that its famed North Course be used for a U.S. Open, but the club continues to decline mostly for privacy reasons.

The San Francisco Golf Club is a mere 25 miles from my home, and I am often privileged to play there as a guest since I have many kind friends who are members. It's always beautifully manicured, has 180 bunkers, and is a true test of golf.

Knowing I had already played a few, I began pondering what it would be like to play all 100. Such an adventure would involve, of course, a lot of hard work, dedication, time and money. I imagined it wouldn't be too difficult a feat if you were a professional player, were involved in some way with the golf business, or were at least retired. In my case none of these qualifications applied. Yet I was definitely interested.

Soon, I was reading the list on almost a daily basis, considering the geography and travel that would be involved and the tactics I could possibly use to gain access to the many private clubs, especially those here in the U.S. I also had to consider the time away from Cathy, time away from my business, and the degree of travel since I now, most likely, would be going solo. In addition, I also had the question of when I could expect to achieve my goal. How many years would it take? After all, the list is always subject to change, and new rankings come out every other September.

After several discussions with Cathy, I arrived at a decision to play the Top 100 Golf Courses in the World. Next to loving Cathy and enjoying good health, this new goal would be paramount in my life.

Of course, I had to set some conditions. For starters, completion of play would fall within the current rankings. For example, if I finished the Top 100 in March 2004, it would be for the current ranking, September 2003 through September 2005. Secondly, in the true spirit of the game, I would walk every course, carrying my own bag unless a caddie was mandatory. Finally, upon completion of my quest, I would put together some sort of journal of my memories with the hope of possibly being able to write a book. I set fall of 2005 as my target date for completing the quest. At that point, I would be 68 years old.

Having played all of the British Open venues, I felt it was appropriate to finish the slate in regard to courses in Great Britain. There were, of course, many other great courses that at the time had not hosted an Open championship. My goal would be to start in England and then head to Portugal, Spain, and France. Considering my age, I thought it best to concentrate on knocking out the overseas courses first if I had a choice. I had previously had my foot problem and my quick bout with cancer. I knew that anything could strike at any time.

After arriving at Heathrow in the spring of 1999, I first went to play at the Sunningdale Golf Club, which

One Man's Opinion

Most Urban Course
Los Angeles Country Club
Miracle Mile in Beverly Hills

Best Clubhouse
Los Angeles
Perfection

Most Unpretentious Locker Room
San Francisco
Like my high school locker room

Shortest Trip for One Round
San Francisco
50 miles

Best Café at the Turn
Sunningdale
Great spot to take a breather

Worst Bag Tag
Ganton
There are none

Best Hospitality
Ganton
An experience to remember

Best Logo
Wicker baskets, Merion
One of a kind

sits just outside the southwest area of London. A gorgeous, very private venue, Sunningdale features two courses, the Old Course and the New Course. To my astonishment, one of the chaps who joined me on the Old Course had a large sheepdog with him. The dog followed us throughout the round, not once making a sound or interfering with play. The dog even knew that the fairways, greens and bunkers were off-limits! After our round, we headed in for a bite and a few single malts. Then it was back to my room for rest. Another day was coming and that meant more golf.

The day after playing Sunningdale, I had a scheduled round at nearby Walton Heath Golf Club. Founded in 1903, Walton Heath also housed an Old Course and a New Course. What first struck me about Walton Heath was that its layout was rather befuddling. One specific area was a spot the locals call "malfunction junction," a term I remembered that once described a section in Knoxville, Tennessee, where several Interstate highways and freeways dumped into city streets with no continuation through town. Walton Heath's "malfunction junction" wasn't that bad but it did feature four holes crossing one another. While I planned to walk myself, I knew right away that I would need a caddie to help me get through the maze of holes and flying golf balls. Another interesting facet of Walton Heath was its ownership. When I was there, the club owned a lease on the tee boxes and greens while the county owned the balance of the layout.

So far, my trip was going exactly as planned. I

was averaging a course a day. The only shopping I did was in the pro shops, while my only sightseeing occurred on the course or on the way to the courses. I began to feel like I was indeed on a quest. My days consisted of checking in, sleeping, playing golf, eating, checking out, and then driving or flying to my next destination. All the while, thinking about Cathy back home.

Moving on, my next stop was Woodhall Spa Golf Club, which is located in the heart of Lincolnshire south of York in northeast England. Home to the Bracken and newly renamed Hotchkin courses, Woodhall was yet another treat. Despite being set inland, Woodhall was a great venue. It was in a lot of ways like a U.S.-style parkland course. Yet somehow it still had a links feel. The course is also home to the National Golf Centre, a golf training school that attracts some of the best young players in Europe.

That same afternoon, following my round and lunch at Woodhall Spa, I was off to Ganton Golf Club, also south of York, for what would be an extremely memorable round and post-golf event.

While planning my trip, I had found out that many of my golfing buddies and colleagues back home had never heard of Ganton. Arriving at the course, I was greeted by an unpaved road that led to a simplistic-looking clubhouse with an unpaved parking lot. I was a little early for my noon tee-time, but went ahead to check in. At the desk, the staff told me they would call for me when my tee-time was set or possibly later. In the meantime, I killed the time practicing on the putting green and shopping in the pro shop. What struck me the most was that in all of my travels this was the first golf club that didn't offer bag tags. Not even for members. When I asked the fellow in the pro shop why they didn't carry bag tags, he simply responded "Why should we? We all know each other."

During my chat with the pro shop staff, the starter came in and asked me if I would please follow him to the starters' shack. I said "Certainly" with some wariness. Had something gone wrong? Had I done something wrong? Would I even be able to play?

As I was told, the club that day was hosting a one-day tournament squaring former Ganton club captains against visiting former Royal Lytham club captains. Captains in the United Kingdom are the same as club presidents in the United States.

It was the 46th rendition of the event, and one of the Royal Lytham members had failed to show up. The secretary of the club asked me if I would like to play in his place. After catching my breath and my racing mind, I told him, "I'm just an average golfer and don't care to interfere with the tournament, but if it's okay with all parties I would love to join you." After a quick response of "Fine," the secretary introduced me to the rest of my foursome and off we went—the former club captains and me, Mr. Average. It was magical! Along with our foursome, there were nine others. I even managed to play a solid round despite the fact that not long after we teed off, a cold and heavy squall swept in from the North Sea and blanketed the course.

Still smiling from ear to ear, I went into the club-house afterwards and washed up, thanking everyone I could. It had truly been, and remains, one of the highlights of my golfing career. Then, just about as I was to leave, Mr. Brown, Ganton's current club captain, approached me and asked if I had a jacket and a tie. If so, I would be welcome to join the two teams for a post-tournament celebration in the club-house. I'd packed a jacket and tie but I'd left them at the bed and breakfast where they couldn't help me anytime soon. I explained my situation and Mr. Brown, the captain, said that it was a shame, but I had to wear a jacket and tie in the clubhouse. He thanked me again for participating, and I was on my way. Or so I thought.

After saying my goodbyes, I was at the door of my car when Mr. Brown came running out of the clubhouse towards me. "Mr. Wentz, you realize our fine club is 107 years old, and to my knowledge has never broken tradition. Then again, the club secretary and I just changed the rules and protocol for the next two hours in order that you might join us without having to wear a jacket and tie. If you would care to join the celebration, you are welcome."

I graciously accepted the generous offer and joined the celebration, which was held in a small bar room decorated with over 100 years of golf memorabilia that consisted of pictures, plaques, trophies, and names of past champions for many, many years. Entering the room, I was greeted as "the jacketless American who filled in for that bastard from Lytham who never showed."

After lengthy fraternizing, many shared laughs and the presentation of awards, I was formally introduced to the group. After my introduction, one chap, who had obviously imbibed a bit too much, stood up and made a toast finishing with, "I hope that bastard who Mr. Wentz had to fill in for will have the courtesy to buy Mr. Wentz a jacket." Just then, another Ganton member stood up and finished a toast by saying, "He should also pay for Mr. Wentz' trip back to San Francisco." On that note, my day at Ganton came to a close. I couldn't wait to get back to my inn and call Cathy.

After a good night of recollections and sleep, I packed my suitcase—especially my jacket and tie!— and headed north to Scotland for more golf at Loch Lomond. Following a few days stay at Loch Lomond, I also made a return trip to Turnberry. By then, the Ailsa Course at Turnberry had become one of my favorites. Turnberry is a mere 50 miles from Glasgow. From Glasgow, I flew home.

Back from my latest trip across the ocean, in the fall of 1999, I briefly hung up my clubs. It was now football season, and always faithful, I decided to take a trip to Columbus, Ohio, where I would watch my UCLA Bruins play Ohio State. In past trips, I had always anxiously bided my time with fellow alumni and university staff. This time, though, I was a bit sidetracked. It was my quest. If possible, I wanted every trip to include at least a few rounds of golf, especially rounds on Top 100 courses.

For this specific trip, where I would again be joined by Brad, both UCLA and Ohio State's athletic departments had agreed that board members coming from California would be offered two days of golf at The Golf Club in New Albany, Ohio, just outside of Columbus as well as golf at Ohio State's Scarlet home course, which held considerable notoriety because it was the course where Jack Nicklaus played as a young Buckeye.

Having access to these two golf courses sparked an impromptu plan to play two more Top 100 courses, Merion Golf Club and Oakmont Country Club, which were located in neighboring eastern and western Pennsylvania respectively. Brad called a friend who was the head professional at a golf course in Monterey, California, and sought his assistance. It was both a long distance telephone call and a long shot. But in the end it proved, as the saying goes, to be worth a shot. Brad's friend came through— we were indeed able to get on both courses.

With a full schedule—golf, football, golf—now set, Brad and I hopped a plane to Philadelphia where we would start our trek with a round at Merion. Designed by Hugh Wilson in 1912, Merion had previously hosted four U.S. Opens, one of those being the 1950 championship where Ben Hogan won the title only a year after nearly dying in an automobile accident that shattered his pelvis. Arriving for our round on Merion's East Course, we were greeted by the remnants of a hurricane that had recently passed through eastern Pennsylvania. The result was a stifling day of 97 percent humidity. Being from the Bay Area, we were used to regular temperatures around 60 degrees. Sucked dry of energy, I didn't play well. Then again, under perfect conditions I would have struggled. Along with being outwitted by the course, I still recall the pins. At the time, instead of using flags to mark the pins, Merion featured a traditional woven Native American wicker basket atop each pin, which is its logo. In my journeys, this logo is unique in golf and is certainly my favorite.

Following lunch, Brad and I went back to the airport to catch a quick flight to Pittsburgh where we would pick up a car and drive to Oakmont. One of Brad's old fraternity brothers met us at the airport. Buoyed by a delicious steak dinner, we got directions to Oakmont, but because it was late at night, we had to be led to the course by Brad's friend. The next day we played.

Founded in 1903, Oakmont has the reputation of being one of the most penal courses in North America. Stray just a bit off track, and your wheels will start spinning. The most famous hazard at Oakmont is the notorious "Church Pews" bunker located between the fairways of holes No.3 and No.4. Overall, the course has hosted more U.S. Open championships than any other course and will do so again in 2007. One of the most memorable rounds in U.S. championship history occurred at Oakmont in 1963 when Johnny Miller shot a stunning 63 to win the championship.

The day we played, I remember being intimidated as soon as I set foot on the first tee. It was as if the course was saying, "Here I am. If you want a piece of me, go for it." I went ahead, but like many others

The clubhouse of Peachtree Golf Club, which was General Sherman's home during the Civil War.

THE BILL ELDRIDGE ROOM

Bill Eldridge, the golf savvy gentleman waiter at Baltusrol Golf Club.

Statue of Payne Stewart depicting his 1999 U.S. Open championship at Pinehurst No. 2.

Things are rather simple and the golf course is one of the world's best at Sand Hills Golf Club.

Directions are needed at Bethpage (Black)

Please have the monkeys clear the tee box at Durban Country Club, South Africa.

Shriners' founding influence at the entry to Medinah Golf Club.

A fantastic four-some and forecaddie (with cap) with the famous Mt. Fuji in the background at the Gotemba Golf Club, Japan.

Host John Terry-Lloyd and Shelia, the forecaddie without her snake stick at Wild Coast Sun Country Club, South Africa.

Keep your eyes on the golf ball and the signage at Yeamans Hall Country Club, South Carolina.

No. 7, a 470-yard par 4, at Ireland's The European Club is among the World's Greatest 100 holes.

Pre-2004 Ryder Cup at Oakland Hills Country Club with flag at half-mast marking President Reagan's passing.

A final drive down the middle and through the chute at Augusta's 18th tee box deserves a high five from my host.

My host prevents a double bogie at the 18th of Augusta as I complete my top 100 quest.

Host Merrick McQuilling needs only a blue blazer to enter the dining room of Garden City Golf Club.

Fifteen holes at Kauri Cliffs, New Zealand view the Pacfic Ocean, six from cliffs.

All aboard for host Walter Forbes' private flight to Nantucket for a quick 18.

Hole No. 5, a 190 yard par 3 at
Loch Lomond.

Bagpiper in full regalia
leads the gang to dinner
at Loch Lomond.

"Hail, hail, the gang's all here." Our group, players and caddies,
in September, 2005 at Loch Lomond where we celebrated completion
of playing the Top 100.

indeed was overmatched. That day, a young professional who had been playing on a mini-tour was in our foursome. Even he was easily dispatched. The fellow had a great swing and could somewhat handle the fairways, but when it came to Oakmont's fearsome greens, he was blown away.

The day before the football game, we met friends from UCLA and drove towards New Albany for a round at the immaculate The Golf Club, which was designed by Pete Dye in 1967. The Golf Club is unique. Its development was sponsored by a few wealthy gentlemen members who drew up very strict guidelines and rules. The course is male only, with women not permitted on the grounds except for the day before Christmas Eve. Even then, the women are only allowed to visit the pro shop in order to buy their member husbands a Christmas gift. I'm not sure how Cathy would react if I ever became a member.

On Saturday, the game day, we still managed to get in even more golf. With the game slated to kick off under lights, we arranged a quick UCLA foursome and played OSU's Scarlet Course. After that, we sped to the game. Overall, I had another great adventure and could check even more courses off my list. The only real downer was the football game. My Bruins lost.

7

Down Under
and Back Over

By late fall of 1999, I was on my way. However, I knew that in order to complete my quest, I would have to consider some key factors. For starters, my goal was to complete the Top 100 in its current ranking. Because the list changes every two years in the fall, I knew that some courses I played could drop out of the rankings. On the other hand, new courses—ones that I had not played or indeed played but at the time were not ranked—could enter the list. Secondly, I had to consider geography and travel. To improve my efficiency, I would try to cluster courses into specific geographical regions. My thought was to tackle the foreign courses first because of my age and the length of the trips and then attempt to crack the courses here in the States. Third, I would somehow need to find ways to gain access to courses that were private and those that were ultra-private.

With these thoughts in mind, I began making plans for a trip to Australia and New Zealand, followed by a trip to Spain and Portugal. With rare exceptions, my target courses were all somewhat centralized—the sand belt near Melbourne, the North and South Islands of New Zealand, and the coastal regions of Spain and Portugal.

As I had in my first trips to England, Scotland, and Ireland, I tried to simplify things by again consulting with a specialized golf travel agent. After considerable research, I found a New Zealand travel firm based in Redondo Beach, California, that specialized in golf trips to Australia and New Zealand. After several meetings with the travel firm, I settled on a schedule that would include 16 courses, six of which were at the time members of the Top 100 club. Overall, the trip Down Under would consist of 19 days and two countries, including travel time. I was scheduled to arrive in Sydney in March of 2000, which would be a perfect time in regard to temperatures. As for my itinerary, the two partners of the travel agency made a little wager on my timeline and ability to play that many courses. One said I would complete my trip and get in all the golf. The other said I had no chance.

I was soon off on a 13-hour flight from San Francisco to Sydney. The flight was turbulent, which worsened my inability to sleep while flying. When we arrived, the other passengers and I were greeted by the "Beagle Brigade," which consisted of numerous beagle dogs adorned in little jackets sniffing in every direction for any illegal drugs and food.

Having passed that test, I checked into my hotel and took a short nap. That evening I dined with a friend of my daughter's who is a native Aussie. Eight years earlier, we had hosted her at our home in the Bay Area while she was on a tennis tour. After dinner and more chatting, we parted and I went to bed. The clock was ticking.

Awakening the next morning, I immediately set off to play Sydney's Australia Golf Club, which claims to be the oldest course in Australia. While not ranked, it was a fine course to start with and very private. That evening, I capped my first day Down Under by attending a symphony at the famous Sydney Opera House. After that, it was again time to get some rest. I knew things were only just getting started.

The following day I stayed close to Sydney and played golf at New South Wales Golf Club. Designed by renowned architect Dr. Alister MacKenzie in 1928, New South Wales, despite heavy winds and rain, was an enjoyable course that instantly became one of my personal favorites because of its scenery and playability. Situated among sand dunes, the course overlooks Botany Bay and was one of MacKenzie's favorites.

A day later, I was in the air again, this time on an early morning two-hour flight that would take me inland to Adelaide for a quick hotel check-in and golf at Royal Adelaide Golf Club, one of Australia's original courses and the host of numerous Australian Open championships. I teed off with three members, all of whom were physicians.

Rather than wind and rain, the weather was extremely hot. I followed the doctors' orders and imbibed what was the refreshment of choice—ginger beer. I had never tasted ginger beer and every time I turned around, someone was offering me a cupful. Despite the heat, it was a pleasant round, but again I had to move on.

A mere day after arriving in Adelaide, I was in the air again, this time headed to Melbourne and National Golf Links, the largest private golf club in Australia. National was where I would make my home for the next five days while playing six courses. The first two days in Melbourne I played National's North and South Courses. On the third, I played the Yarra Yarra Golf Club. While all three were unranked at the time, it was on the Yarra Yarra course that I got my first Down Under surprise.

When I arrived at Yarra Yarra (which is aboriginal for "flowing, flowing") for my mid-morning round, I was told to mark time while they figured out my tee slot. After a brief time, one of the chaps in the pro shop asked me if I would mind being paired with a handicapped gentleman who would be riding in his small handicap cart while the rest of us walked. Not until midway through the round did I understand, but I again found myself playing in a club tournament. We all had a great time on the course, and again I was invited to a post-tourney celebration in the grandiose clubhouse where a bit more drinking and fraternizing occurred. At one point, my playing partner invited the club president to our table so that I could meet him. Things then immediately changed. When told that I had filled in for a missing player, he commenced to scold my partner over and over, telling him that the tournament was open to members only and that he had broken the code. After some brief discussion, the president discovered that I was an American and was told about my quest. Suddenly, he not only calmed down but also became a gracious host. We spent the next few hours chatting together about great golf courses of the world, the president all the while apologizing to me and my partner for his initial reaction.

A day after my Yarra Yarra experience, I played nearby Kingston Heath Golf Club, first designed by Dan Soutar and later retouched by MacKenzie. The most striking thing to me at Kingston Heath was the speed of the greens. They were the fastest I had yet to play. Another highlight at Kingston Heath was the par three 15th which features a tee shot over basically a wasteland. The hole has been called Australia's best par three. After playing it, I wouldn't contest that claim.

Before wrapping up my Australia stay, I got in rounds on both the East and West Courses at Royal Melbourne Golf Club. Royal Melbourne's world ranking is based on a composite of part of its East Course and part of its West Course. Therefore, it was critical for me to play the identical layout if I were to check it off my list, which I did. This is another MacKenzie-designed gem and is regarded as the oldest and finest venue Down Under. As in Adelaide, the weather was unbearably hot, the temperature hovering over 100 degrees. The heat, however, was the least of my concerns. During my play on the West Course, I went off as a single and unfortunately saw many of my balls fly into the heavy rough. It was during one of my searches that I suddenly recalled an article that I had read previous to my trip that stated, "All snakes in Australia are poisonous. In fact, the world's ten most poisonous snakes call the continent home." As soon as I remembered that, I was done looking for my balls in the brush. I could handle a kangaroo, maybe a koala, but snakes? No thank you.

Following my enjoyable round, I showered, checked out of the hotel, and drove to Melbourne for a night flight that would take me to Christchurch, New Zealand. On my way to the airport, I stopped by the Melbourne Zoo to buy some

> **One Man's Opinion**
>
> Most Difficult Greens
> Oakmont and Kingston Heath (tie)
> *Lightning fast, all 18*

gifts for my grandchildren. Of course, many of the toys were snakes. After a nearly four-hour flight over the Tasman Sea, I landed in Christchurch where the temperature was a cool 42 degrees. What a difference from the 100-degree-plus weather in Melbourne!

Having arrived in the wee hours of the following morning, I was pooped. Still, I had to go through very strict customs, which included inspectors emptying my golf bag and requiring me to wash my two pairs of golf shoes. They were very concerned about things—snakes, critters, food and contaminated soil—coming into their country from Australia. This delay took so long that all public transportation had shut down for the night. I was forced to hitch a ride with an airport employee who took me to my hotel. When I finally lay down, it was 4 a.m. My tee-time for my next round, which was to be played at Christchurch Golf Club, was 8 a.m.

Still exhausted, I got in my round at Christchurch, which, while unranked, had its charm. Originally founded in 1873, the Christchurch club is the second oldest course in New Zealand. Its clubhouse and surroundings display its history magnificently. After my round, I headed straight back to the hotel for lunch and rest. During lunch, I picked up a newspaper that had a half-page headline exclaiming, "Brown Snake Discovered in Container from Adelaide." A sub-headline stated, "Search Continues for Snake Eggs." Snakes! I thought I was done with snakes. There are no known snakes in New Zealand and the natives certainly don't want them.

Fully rested, I traveled the next few days to play two more unranked courses on the south island, Millbrook Golf Resort and Kelvin Heights Golf Course. I then flew north to New Zealand's capital, Wellington, to play Wellington Golf Club, which was also unranked but like the others a great venue. The next morning I drove north through very stormy weather to play Paraparaumu Beach Golf Club. Lucky for me, by the time I was to play Paraparaumu, the weather had cleared and was beautiful. The course, a regular host of the New Zealand Open, is regarded as one of the country's best links courses and is indeed quite rugged.

Situated on the Kapiti Coast, Paraparaumu is links golf at its best. Stray anywhere off the fairway and you are greeted by menacing bunkers and sloping lies. Because the course is situated on the coast, the wind is ever-present. For me, a lover of links-style golf, Paraparaumu was a beauty. The only blemish on the day was that when I was ready to leave, I discovered that the battery in my rental car was dead. I had apparently never turned off my lights after driving through the morning's storm. I visited the golf course superintendent, whom I had met earlier in the day, to see if he could help somehow.

He charged my battery and left saying, "Have a safe trip but remember to keep the engine running for a while until the battery is again fully charged."

"Fine and thanks again," I replied as I looked to head out.

Then I saw that my gas tank was nearly empty. I still had a six-hour drive north to Lake Taupo and my next lodging. At my earliest convenience, I found a service station and filled up with the engine running before heading on my way.

Finally arriving at my destination, I checked in, grabbed some quick desk candies, which I shouldn't do, and headed straight for the bar. The weather was hot and I desperately needed something cool to drink. While standing at the bar, I realized that there was something weird happening in my mouth. While chewing on the candies at the check-in desk, I had loosened a full gold crown on one of my teeth, enough that it came out. My mind began racing. What do I do? Will it be painful or will the tooth possibly chip? I was to play my last course early the next day before flying home again. What to do?

Instantly ignoring my thirst, I went back to the check-in area, told the receptionist my story and asked if she or anyone else knew of a local dentist that I could call. She did, and I was right back in the car headed to the dentist's office. A young female dentist, who just happened to be working late, reset my crown for a fee of 46 U.S. dollars. I was back at the hotel within 45 minutes, and when I went to the bar, my drink was still there. "Where'd you go?" the bartender asked. I replied, "Oh, I just went to have some quick dental work done." He replied, "Well then, I'll freshen it up and it's on the house." It was one of the most satisfying drinks of my life.

When I got to my room, I found a message from my next day's host asking me to call him no matter the hour. Something was going on with our tee-time. As with other occasions, the thought crossed my mind that maybe our round was cancelled. After reaching him, I learned that there had indeed been some sort of a mix-up regarding the next day's planned play at Wairakei, but I was still to be at the course early in the morning in case something changed.

The following morning, refreshed and wearing my newly set crown, I arrived at the course at 6:30 a.m. and met my host, John Lister, who happened to be a former professional. The problem, was that a New Zealand Senior PGA Pro-Am tournament was scheduled that day; however, he had a plan that he felt would work. For the tournament, one half of the field was to start shortly at 8 a.m. at No.1, with the other half starting at No.10. He proposed that I tee off immediately at No.1 as a single before the tournament got under way. By the time I reached No.10, he reasoned, I could stop in for a sandwich or something and then follow the last foursome of the tournament that would be teeing off on No.10. I agreed and went off No.1 as a single.

Later, when I arrived at the 10th tee I saw that the Pro-Am teams were backed up a bit. While I mingled around the tee area, a player in the tournament, the club pro from Royal Melbourne, recognized me from my previous week's visit to his club. He asked why I was just hanging around and what I was doing at Wairakei. After I explained my situation he quickly replied, "Why don't you just join our foursome and play the back-nine with us?" Here I was once again playing amid some kind of tournament, but this was not a normal tournament for it was my first Pro-Am even though it was only for nine holes.

As was the case following other events in which I played, I was invited to join the post-tournament festivities. I continuously found during my quest that if you are traveling as a single, you are invited into certain social circles a lot more than if there were others. It's just a matter of numbers. Between laughs, a couple of beers and food, I was presented with a New Zealand Pro-Am golf cap with a Kiwi logo just like I was one of the boys. It was again a great time, but unfortunately I had to run because I still faced a long drive north to Auckland for the next day's flight back to the States.

Despite a Down Under schedule that was tight, I

achieved my goals. The one travel agent had lost his bet. The highlight of Australia and New Zealand was simply the people. They seemed to really love life, were always in a good mood, and loved sports of any kind. Admittedly though, I was exhausted. When Cathy met me at the airport after my arrival back home, she asked if I would ever take such a time-constrained trip again. "The next time I'm 21 years old," I replied with a smile.

After a few months, I was on the move again. The other half of my 2000 schedule included a fall trip to Spain and Portugal followed by a brief return to Scotland to play my favorites. On the mainland of Europe, there were three ranked courses that I had yet to play plus three unranked courses. Knowing that my daughter had never been to Spain or Portugal, I asked her to join me. Because of her job schedule, she would indeed come to Spain and Portugal, but then she would fly back home while I went on to Scotland.

Time flew by, and we were soon on our way. After landing in Barcelona, we drove southwest to the Mediterranean coast to Valencia, home of El Saler Golf Club. Unfortunately, a heavy storm hit and I had to cancel my round. It was the first time that one of my planned rounds had to be cancelled. Moving on, we proceeded a bit farther down the coast to Marbella where I got in rounds at a pair of unranked venues, Sotogrande Golf Club and Torrequebrada Golf Club. Sotogrande was the first course renowned architect Robert Trent Jones Sr. ever built in Spain, while Torrequebrada was a former host course for the Spanish Open.

I then paid a visit to the queen of Spanish golf, Valderrama Golf Club. Also designed by Trent Jones Sr., Valderrama, in 1997, hosted the annual Ryder Cup and continues to be one of Europe's greatest golf tracks. It is a magnificent venue along the Mediterranean Sea and plays very fair. Overall, five sets of tees can be played, making the course a treat for all levels of play. Two holes that really stood out were the par four 16th and the par four 18th. While short in length, the 16th features an uphill drive that demands accuracy. Miss your shot and the length of the hole increases by fathoms. No.18, meanwhile, is a dogleg left hole that ranks as one of the best finishing holes in golf.

Following my round at Valderrama, my daughter and I hopped back in the car and drove to the Algarve region of Portugal where I was to play unranked Quinta Golf Club and San Lorenzo Golf Club. My main target was San Lorenzo, then a ranked course, but now it has fallen off the charts. Still, it was a beautiful venue, a tough course sitting along the shoreline of the Mediterranean and nestled near the Ria Formosa Nature Reserve.

After our visit to Portugal, it was time for Julie to go home. With one more day left together, we decided to take a quick hovercraft boat trip from Gibraltar across the Mediterranean Sea to Morocco. While in Morocco, we visited the bazaars and watched the locals tantalize cobras with their music, did some sightseeing, and returned that evening to Spain.

At the airport the following day, Julie left for the States and I left for Scotland for return visits to my favorite Scottish courses—Loch Lomond, Turnberry, and Muirfield. It was following a round at Muirfield that I met and began conversing with two fellow Americans who were in Europe working on the development of a new golf club. After telling them about my quest, they became very interested and we exchanged business cards. They told me to give them a call as soon as I got home. They apparently had connections at some of the private American courses that I had yet to visit, primarily in the Northeast.

On the flight home, I realized that meeting the two men could be a good start. At some point, I knew I would really have to network. Overall, it had been a great year. In 2000, I had played 23 foreign courses, six of which were part of my quest. I had been in five different countries and had played on the shores of six different bodies of water—the Pacific Ocean, the Tasman Sea, the Mediterranean Sea, the Atlantic Ocean, the Irish Sea, and the North Sea.

No doubt about it, my quest was in full swing.

8

It's a Post 9/11 World

W hen I officially began my quest, my list of the Top 100 courses included 42 foreign courses and 58 courses in the United States, with the American courses comprising primarily private courses. As a result, I knew I had to start networking to find ways onto to those member-only venues, which was to become the most difficult challenge of my quest. In my early trips around the globe, I had learned that it was always a good idea to be open to people and let them know what I was trying to do, yet not overdo it. Once people heard about my quest, they generally became interested and most wanted to help me any way they could, especially fellow golfers.

As I reviewed the list in making plans for 2001, I saw that a number of target courses were located in the New England region. The State of New York, in fact, had an amazing 10 courses on the list, and after having played them, I felt that all belonged there. A brief review made the conclusion easy. I would wait for the weather to cool a bit and head east in the late summer. With so many courses located within the same basic proximity, I could arrange an easy trip if I did it right. As a bonus, I also planned a quick trip to watch the Ryder Cup, which was being held at The Belfry Course in England later in the fall.

First, however, I would kick off the new season by taking a trip to Las Vegas with Cathy. We hadn't been there for over two decades, and we wouldn't have to fly. We could drive this one. Cathy was all for it and off we went.

With Cathy again at my side, our first golf destination when we arrived in Las Vegas that May was Shadow Creek Golf Course, a Tom Fazio-designed layout that since its inception in 1989 has become one of golf's finest. Located just a short drive off the Vegas Strip, Shadow Creek makes you wonder how such a paradise could be located in what is mostly a vast wasteland. The course features spectacular waterfalls, simulated rocks and incredible foliage including fresh pine needles imported annually from North Carolina. While a bit pricey, Shadow Creek is a must if you're a diehard golfer staying in Vegas. It's simply an amazing venue, notably reminiscent of a Disneyland creation and a testament to man making something out of nothing.

Following our trip to Sin City, we drove to Los Angeles where I performed some duties for the board of trustees of UCLA. Then we returned to the Bay Area where I would continue planning my New

England and Ryder Cup ventures. For my fall trip, I was considering a number of Long Island courses, including Maidstone Golf Club, Shinnecock Hills Golf Club, National Golf Links of America, Bethpage Golf Course and Garden City Golf Club. Overall, five ranked courses on Long Island alone. The key to playing the Long Island courses was that the courses were located within approximately 90 miles of each other.

The first course I tried to check off my list was Maidstone Golf Club. Founded in 1891, Maidstone is one of the oldest golf courses in the U.S. However, because the course was private I first had to focus on securing access. I made every effort before my trip to find a connection. After many phone calls, I finally made contact with a Maidstone member through a friend of mine at Pebble Beach who knew the member. As my trip loomed, I had networked rounds at both Shinnecock Hills and Maidstone. But I still had much work to do. Among my main targets was also a visit to Bethpage Golf Course, which was set to host the 2002 U.S. Open. Even being a

One Man's Opinion

Most Unnatural Course
Shadow Creek
The art of creation in the desert

Most Expensive Round
Shadow Creek
$500 in 2001

Best Course
Shinnecock Hills
If I could play only one more

Best Bar
Shinnecock Hills
Jefferson's Bar and the green wicker chairs

Most Desired Membership
Shinnecock Hills
A nonresident opening please

public course, Bethpage was notorious as a venue where you had to simply wait your turn, which meant even sleeping in your car to secure a tee-time.

My plan was that I had a member-host arrangement set up for both Maidstone and Shinnecock. I had nothing set up for the National Golf Club, and I would just wait in line at Bethpage like everyone else. Also, I had a network plan in progress for Garden City but hadn't heard anything definite.

Challenged but undaunted, I left in mid-August of 2001, on a flight that would take me from San Francisco to New York City. I arrived to a typical hot and humid East Coast day. My goal was to play at least two of the ranked courses. Leaving the airport, I headed directly for the east end of Long Island to my simple motel room in Southampton and then on to meet my Maidstone member-host. Maidstone, designed by somewhat forgotten architect Willie Parks Jr., has a tough links layout with plenty of scrub areas and hazards, including a pond and a marsh waiting to suck up your ball, which I happily avoided. Every shot in your bag has to be played at

---

One Man's Opinion

Hardest Public Course to Get On
Bethpage Black Course
Bring your sleeping bag

Least Expensive Round
Bethpage Black Course
$34 in 2001

Best Score
Quaker Ridge
74 gross, sixth straight day of golf

Best Pro Shop
Baltusrol
A haberdashery with golf balls

Best Personality
Bill Eldridge, Baltusrol
Greatest waiter ever

Maidstone. Following the round, my member-host, his son, and I watched the conclusion of the 2001 PGA Championship in the locker room.

After leaving Maidstone, I was scheduled to meet Eugene Zuriff and his wife Sherrie. Eugene was the individual who had arranged my playing at Maidstone. For two days, I was the guest of Eugene and his wife. The two were fantastic hosts and further hosted me at the Atlantic Golf Club with his business associate Alan Stillman and at the Noyac Golf Club, two fine private courses on Long Island.

While visiting with the Zuriffs, I met two other house guests who hailed from Paris. Of course, my quest came up in discussions, and they were all eager to help. One of the guests, in fact, asked if any courses on the list were in his homeland. When I told him that the only one was Morfontaine Golf Club, he exclaimed that he was a member and that next time I was in Paris I should contact him. The networking that I knew I had to somehow accomplish was coming together.

Following my stay with the Zuriffs, I arrived at the prestigious Shinnecock Hills Golf Club to meet my host. Because I had never met the fellow before, I made sure I was prompt. Again, the air was hot and sticky and difficult for a Californian to relate to. In the morning before meeting my host, I remembered that the superintendent at Shinnecock Hills was Mark Michaud. Earlier in his career, Mark had been the superintendent at Pebble Beach Golf Links. During his time there, I had got to know him well enough that one year I hosted him and other members of the Pebble Beach staff for golf and dinner at Los Angeles Country Club. Mark had also more than once returned our dogs when they got free and roamed around the Pebble Beach course.

While speaking with Mark, he asked why I was there, which member I was playing with, and where I was headed after Shinnecock Hills. I told him that I was hoping to play National Golf Links and Bethpage (Black Course) before heading back home, but that I had no confirmed tee-times. I mentioned that I was doubtful about getting in a round at National Golf Links, but that I had a good feeling about Bethpage because the course is public and thus more accessible. He said, "It'll be difficult to play Bethpage and the others on such short notice, but I could possibly help you on a return trip." Mark also said, "Could you maybe return this October? That could be a good time."

As I listened fervently, he went on to tell me that at that time I could possibly replay Shinnecock and gain access to both Bethpage and National. My mind spinning, I immediately replied, "Well, sounds like I'll see you in October."

October was a mere two months away, and I hadn't planned another trip. Yet it was an opportunity I just couldn't pass up. After my talk with Mark, my member-host and I played the Shinnecock Hills course, which as I expected turned out to be a very difficult test of golf. Years later while watching the 2005 U.S. Open at the course, I could easily understand why so many of the world's greatest players struggled. It's just tough, pure golf at its best.

Following my day at Shinnecock Hills, I headed a

tad west on Long Island towards Bethpage Golf Course. I was set to fly home in two days. Even though I had chatted with Mark about getting on the busy public course, I still thought I would roll the dice. While examining Bethpage during my planning, I had seen numerous articles regarding the difficulty of getting onto Bethpage's Black Course. The course was set to host the 2002 U.S. Open the following summer, and its popularity was skyrocketing. While planning my trip, I had called every possible phone number and linked with every possible website. I even wrote letters to the course asking if someone could tell me the specific process for a non-New York resident to get a tee-time. The only clear response in helping was being told that if I had a current New York ID card I would be a leg up.

The day I planned to play, I popped out of bed in the wee morning hours. My goal was to be at the starter's area at 3:30 a.m. Arriving at the course, I quickly saw that the media weren't joking about people spending the night in their cars to play the course. A line of wannabe Black Course golfers of all stripes and sizes had already formed. They passed the waiting time by smoking and drinking and gambling under the moonlight. I waited until 10 a.m. but missed the cut as a single. Still hopeful, I tried again the next morning. This time I arrived at 5:30 a.m. Again, I was shut out at 10 a.m. as a single. I began thinking about the possibilities of acquiring a New York ID card, yet quickly came to my senses. I would head home and give it another shot later in October, following the advice of Mark.

After a few weeks back home in the Bay Area, I was set to take off again. Not for a return trip to New York, but to England where I was slated to watch the Ryder Cup at The Belfry.

Then the tragedy of September 11, 2001, occurred. Immediately, the Ryder Cup was cancelled as was my trip. The country that I call home had been attacked by a group of rogue terrorists. In a single day, America had changed forever.

The airlines situation was now a bit shaky even for me. Cathy and I decided instead to drive north to Oregon where we would get in rounds at Pacific Dunes Golf Course and Bandon Dunes Golf Course. While I had wanted to see the Ryder Cup, the Oregon trip was special because Cathy was again with me. As a bonus, we could also take our two terriers—Abbie and Bogey.

At the time, both Pacific Dunes and Bandon Dunes were relatively new courses that had quickly jumped onto the list of the World's Top 100 Golf Courses. I played the first round of the Oregon leg of my quest on Pacific Dunes, which had opened earlier that year. Then it was a round at Bandon Dunes, which was designed by David McLay Kidd. While Cathy walked the dogs on the beach, I made my way through both links-style courses. Had someone blindfolded me and dropped me off in the middle of either course, my first thought would be that I was somewhere in Scotland. I, of course, was in Oregon. To add to the magic, while I played Bandon Dunes, the rain poured and the winds kicked up. The only thing missing at both venues was the sound of bagpipes reverberating in the distance. To this day, Bandon Dunes to me typifies golf in Scotland more than any other U.S. course.

A month later, even with the fear of flying and schedule uncertainties, I returned to Long Island to pick up my quest from the previous two months. Through some fortunate networking and a bit of luck, the trip had grown to be seven courses of the World's Top 100 Golf Courses to be played in a mere eight days.

I would start the trip by arriving in Newark, New Jersey, to play nearby Baltusrol Golf Club followed by Shinnecock Hills again, then National Golf Links, another try at Bethpage, and then over to Garden City. From there, I would head to the west end of Long Island to Westchester County to play Winged Foot (West) and Quaker Ridge. It was quite a plan.

Back home at my home course, Menlo Country Club, the course superintendent, Scott Lewis, whom I knew, had a member of his crew whose father, Jim Stark, was a member of Baltusrol. Jim would eventually get me onto nine of the ranked courses, more than anyone.

At Baltusrol, Jim met me. My stay at Baltusrol was terrific, yet sadness was still in the air from the previous month's 9/11 tragedy just across the river. While checking into my room at the club, both the manager and his secretary had told me that on the fateful day they had both stood on the deck of my room where on the horizon they saw the Twin Towers burn and eventually collapse. In addition, the two other players in our foursome were a father and son. The son, who worked on Wall Street, had lost his best friend in the attack. The two regularly shared a commuter train that took him to Wall Street and his friend to the World Trade Center. All of the stories were extremely sad and put my quest in perspective.

On the positive side, my stay, the golf, and meeting Jim for the first time made things a bit brighter. During my stay, I had also met Bill Eldridge, a guy who brings a smile to one and all, no matter the situation. While rather quiet, Bill, a waiter at the Baltusrol club, knew tons of golf stories, and seemed to have visited with everyone who had ever played golf. In addition to his repertoire of golf stories he also wrote poetry. In my worldwide quest I never met anyone as unique as Bill.

After a great time, I was soon on my way again, this time heading east towards Southampton for my return visit to Shinnecock Hills. The following morning, I got in my second round at Shinnecock Hills, following that with an afternoon round at National Golf Links of America. Literally next door to Shinnecock Hills, National Golf Links of America is another one of America's grandest golf courses. First opened in 1911, as a creation of architect Charles Blair MacDonald, National Golf Links was designed in the style of Scotland and England's greatest old courses. MacDonald wanted a course that would survive the test of time.

That evening, I went to bed early in preparation for taking my third shot at getting onto the Bethpage Golf Course (Black Course). The good news this time was that I wouldn't have to get up in the middle of the night to wait in line with countless others. Thanks to Mark Michaud, I had a tee-time at 10 a.m. Nevertheless, I knew I had to be at the course early. As it turned out, the third time was indeed the charm. I got to the course at about 8 a.m., proceeded to hit some balls on the range, stood in line, paid my green fee of a mere $34, and was off to the starter right on time. Since my last visit, the course had initiated a new system whereby when you pay your green fee, a member of the course staff puts a small plastic bracelet around your wrist with all of your information on it similar to what you are issued at a hospital. When you get to the starter, he matches your bracelet information with his daily sheet. If all information matches, you are free to play the course.

After being cleared, I made my way to the first tee where I saw something I'd never seen before at any course. There, in almost blazing letters, was a sign that read, "The Black Course is an Extremely Difficult Golf Course Which We Recommend Only for Highly Skilled Golfers." Overall, there are five (Yellow, Green, Blue, Red and Black) courses at Bethpage that each cater to different levels of play. I had yet to tee off, yet I was already beginning to feel intimated. I'm sure I was not the only one who has felt that way after seeing the Black Course warning sign.

While a bit daunted, I still went out to experience what was a pleasurable round. I carried my bag and although the course was very difficult, it was a joy. At the time of my round, the course was already preparing for the upcoming 2002 U.S. Open. During my round and my visit, I continually asked the locals how they thought the pros would fare on such a long and hard track. The overwhelming response was that no one would break par. They were nearly correct. When the Open did arrive in June of 2002, only one player—champion Tiger Woods—would crack the magical red numbers line.

As it was at Baltusrol and the other New York courses, the banter of club members was restrained by the shocking events of September 11. Back home in California, there was a tide of patriotism. In New York, there was a flood. Almost everywhere you looked, Old Glory flapped in the wind, flowers and signs exclaimed "God Bless America," and "United We Stand." What a sad reminder of what had happened, but also what a testament to the spirit and resolve of America.

After play at Bethpage, I called my host to confirm play for tomorrow's round at Garden City. Unfortunately, and with great regrets, he asked if I could take a rain check and possibly reschedule play for a future date. Garden City is an elite, all-male club and he said that 9/11 had claimed the lives of 32 of its members and it seemed like every day he was attending a memorial service. I certainly understood the situation and continued my drive to Winged Foot. Along the way, I saw nothing but signs, flowers and American flags.

I continued on to Mamaroneck, New York, where I got in a round at Winged Foot Golf Club

(West Course), thanks to Kenneth Gestal and Walter Forbes. Another one of A.W. Tillinghast's masterpieces, Winged Foot's West Course most recently hosted the 2006 U.S. Open. It is another long and deadly track. I started my day at the course very early with the hopes of playing both the West and East Courses, each of which were on my rankings list. I ended up playing the West Course. With darkness quickly approaching I was not able to play both courses in one day. Hopefully, my host would invite me back at some time when I could then play the East Course. One course in one day at Winged Foot was enough. The West Course, as Phil Mickelson and Scotsman Colin Montgomerie found out in the 2006 U.S. Open, is just waiting to kill your scorecard. You have to be on your toes all 18 holes, every stroke of the way.

My last open day in the New York area, I lucked out. I hadn't planned on getting in any golf, but my son Brad back home had made some quick phone calls to an old University of Arizona friend of his who had a connection at Quaker Ridge Golf Club, which is contiguous to Winged Foot. After a night full of phone calls, I was able to get on Quaker Ridge without a host present. Yet again, the course was an A.W. Tillinghast design and it is a gem. Legend has it that George Washington once slept under a tree that now sits on the 10th hole.

Helping me along was my caddie, whose name was Joey. Joey, like many other caddies I had, was an instant favorite. He knew the course and much of its storied past, everything from the course's

Revolutionary War history to Quaker Ridge's hosting of its first major, the 1936 Metropolitan Open, which was won by Byron Nelson in a field that included legendary golfers Gene Sarazen, Paul Runyon, and Tommy Armour. Quaker Ridge, built in 1916 and nicknamed "Tillie's Treasure," remains virtually unchanged today.

After the round, I went back to my room and collapsed. I had achieved the majority of my goal, yet I knew there was much more to come. My quest was close to half-way finished.

CHAPTER

9

Going South

As a result of the events of September 11, my quest had definitely taken a turn. As I made my plans for the 2002 season, the tragedy was still fresh in my mind. Yet, if I planned to complete my goal, I knew I had to forge on. I realized that the contacts that I had previously made may not always be there. I had to take advantage of my past networking as soon as I could.

As I looked ahead, my immediate thought was that I should head to the South where I could get in rounds at courses in both the Carolina and Florida regions. Looking at my list, I saw that several ranked courses were public. Another positive feature was the weather. I thought that even if I left during the winter, I more than likely wouldn't be affected by cold weather. My plan was to start as far south as possible, working my way north before flying back home. The original target included six courses, yet that number could drop to four. During my initial planning, I forgot that the Players Championship was coming up at the Tournament Players Course (TPC) in Sawgrass, Florida. Also, I still hadn't found a way to get on the very private Seminole Golf Club in North Palm Beach.

Nonetheless, I would still take my chances and hope to get in all six courses. My final plan would include an initial visit to Casa de Campo in the Dominican Republic. Then I would fly to Miami and head north to Seminole. Knowing I still had no contact there, I gave myself two extra days with hopes that I would find a way to get on. I would then head north to World Woods, Harbour Town, and Pinehurst before turning around and going southward to Ponte Vedra Beach with hopes of playing the TPC at Sawgrass a mere day after the conclusion of the Players Championship.

Only a week before leaving on my latest sojourn, I still didn't have a member contact for Seminole. I had tried everything I could possibly think of, including talking to every single person I could remember who had at one time lived in or vacationed in Florida. I became so desperate I began asking people who had ever eaten a Florida orange. If there's a will, there's a way. I had the will. I just didn't have the way.

Then I suddenly remembered. A friend of mine, Dr. Charles Young, had taken a temporary position as president of the University of Florida in Gainesville. During my time as a board member at UCLA, I had worked with Dr. Young, who was then the chancellor of UCLA. On occasion, we had played golf together. Hoping that something would still be possible, I fired an e-mail to him explaining my situation and noting that I had set aside two days on my schedule just in case anything was possible. My biggest question, of course, was, "Do you know any members, or a friend of a member, or a friend of a friend of a member?" Amazingly and luckily, I heard from Dr. Young later the same day. "Yes, I can get you on. Which of the two days fits best with your schedule?" I had to pinch myself. Weeks of agony and worry disappeared in a matter of seconds. I was ready to fly, both literally and figuratively.

> **One Man's Opinion**
>
> Best Locker Room
> Seminole
> *One to copy*
>
> Most Obscure Course
> Morfontaine
> *Even hard to find with a member*
>
> Most Understated Clubhouse
> Peachtree
> *Small and quaint*

Thrilled beyond belief, I started my trip right where I wanted to, at Casa de Campo in the Dominican Republic. Designed by Pete Dye, who lives on the course, Casa de Campo's Teeth of the Dog course is the only one in the Caribbean that has ever been a member of the Top 100 list. Nestled against the sea, it features eight breathtaking ocean holes. Interestingly enough, when I got to the resort there was a mini traffic jam with police and onlookers. Turned out, former President Bill Clinton was on the grounds taking his own golf vacation. When things finally settled down a bit, I checked in for my one-night stay. I never did see the President, either on the resort grounds or on the course saying "I'll take a mulligan." I myself teed off early the next morning and was quickly headed back to Miami the same afternoon.

Back in Miami, I drove north that evening to North Palm Beach where the next day I was slated to play Seminole Golf Club. Thanks to Dr. Young, it was really happening! Following the morning round on the Donald Ross-designed course, I joined Dr. Young and other University of Florida alumni and officials who had also played the Seminole course that morning for a delicious lunch in their famous clubhouse. There was an awful lot of conversation regarding the school's athletic program and its fundraising program. Beause we were on the home course of Florida State University, I would have thought there would be some tension. Apparently, the rivalry between the Gators and Seminoles only exists on the playing field.

As on other occasions, I wished I could have stayed and fraternized longer. Seminole had a way of making you feel at home. But I had to move on.

That afternoon, I drove west to settle in for a night's rest before playing an early morning round at World Woods Golf Club (Pine Barrens). One of the most striking things about World Woods is its practice range, which *Sports Illustrated* once dubbed "The best practice facility in the world." Of course, the golf course, which was one of Florida's newest courses, having been founded and designed by Tom Fazio in 1993, is also memorable. Known to some as the "Poor Man's Pine Valley," the course also rests among sandy hills. It was not what I would have expected for Florida golf.

A day and a somewhat lengthy drive later, I found myself at Harbour Town Golf Links, which sits on Hilton Head Island off the coast of South Carolina. Home to the PGA Tour's Heritage Classic, Harbour Town is the cream of golf in South Carolina. A joint Pete Dye/Nicklaus design, the public access course demands accuracy as there are a slew of huge bunkers waiting. At the time of my round, the course was undergoing preparations for that year's Heritage Classic. Hence, it played beautifully, straight away but with very small greens and alligators.

Following my round at Harbour Town, I played an unplanned round at Kiawah Island (Ocean Course), also in South Carolina. The future site of the 2012 PGA Championship, Kiawah Island is another one of architect Pete Dye's latest creations. Set along the shoreline of the island, the Ocean Course was indeed an ocean course with wind a major factor.

The next stop was one of America's greatest venues, Pinehurst No.2 in nearby North Carolina. Designed by legend Donald Ross, Pinehurst has become a staple among courses used for the U.S. Open. It was at the course that the late Payne Stewart struck his magical putt on the green of No.18 to win the 1999 U.S. Open. Today, a full-size bronze statue of Stewart in his famous stance commemorates the occasion. Bobby Jones once called the course the "St. Andrews of U.S. golf courses."

What struck me the most about the layout were the greens. Being crowned, they made putting that much more of an adventure.

Following my round, I went to the lounge area of the hotel to take a breather. The whole area was extremely crowded. As I discovered, the staff members of a national golf magazine were on a retreat. They were waiting for dinner, which was to include a presentation by Tom Fazio. After fraternizing with some of the staff members, I was invited to join them. The dinner was, of course, grand, but getting a chance to listen to Fazio speak was even better. It was the first time I had ever heard someone talk about the game from the perspective of a course designer.

A day after my visit to Pinehurst, I left on a seven-hour drive that would take me back to Florida. The goal was to get in one more round at Sawgrass before flying home. As I was heading out of Pinehurst, I stopped at a small golf shop in the village to see what was for sale. Turned out, the proprietor, had literally just finished framing and matting a collage of 18th-hole flags from the 2000 British Open at St. Andrews, the 2000 U.S. Open at Pebble Beach, the 2001 Masters at Augusta National, and the 2001 PGA Championship at Valhalla—the Tiger Slam! What made the piece even more appealing was that Tiger Woods had signed each flag and there was verification and insurance for the signatures. It was an awesome sight. When the proprietor said he could ship to California, the deal was done. The collage remains one of my greatest golf treasures and a fantastic conversation piece.

I arrived later that evening in Ponte Vedra Beach and went straight into my routine of checking in, eating dinner, and then immediately going to bed knowing that I would have to get up early for the next day's golf. Amazingly, at The Players Club at Sawgrass, I was in the first group to go out that day, a two-some. Less than 24 hours before, golf's greatest players had walked the fairways in hopes of winning the prestigious The Players Championship. The grandstands and TV towers from the previous week's action were still standing, and the rough was just starting to be mowed for normal play. The greens, as I found out, were still playing awfully fast. My partner for the round was a young fellow who could definitely play. While he was playing, he was on his cell phone every other hole talking to his young golfing buddies in his Atlanta office, where they were betting over and under on his results. Thing was, because he took a cart while I walked the course, we didn't actually talk much until we were both on the green. Inevitably, we eventually both found ourselves on the tee area of the famous 17th island hole. As we stood there, the two nearest maintenance men who had been shaving the rough turned off their mowers. In complete silence, we both looked across the water at a pin that seemed as far away as Cuba. My playing partner and I agreed that we would count our first shot, but that we each would be allowed one extra free shot to reach the green. There was no one behind us, and we both shared the same opinion that this could possibly be the last time we ever played the hole.

At the time, the pin was about eight feet from

the collar of the green, set at 7 o'clock. My first and second shot found their way onto the green, while my partner's first ball hit the green. I'll leave you to guess where his second shot ended up. Counting our first balls only, we both went on to make par, myself two-putting from about nine feet out. I had made par on No.17 at Sawgrass! On the flight back home to San Francisco later that evening, that was all I could think about. I had conquered one of golf's most difficult and treacherous holes, even though it obviously would be a different story had there been a gallery, TV cameras, and money on the line.

My 2002 season was off and running. I had checked off all of my intended targets in the South, even getting in my round at Seminole and an unscheduled round at Kiawah Island. After return-ing home, I made plans for another venture, this time another trip across the Atlantic. Because my daughter Julie had never been to Scandinavia and wanted to go, I agreed that she could join me. We left in May, starting out with visits to both Sweden and Norway. Being of Norwegian descent, we espe-cially enjoyed Norway. Apparently, Julie with her blue eyes and blonde hair fit in so well that she was-n't even asked for her passport at the airport. As I recall, the attendant simply said, "Please go through. I can tell you live here."

After leaving Norway, we flew to London where Julie caught a flight back home to the States. Like our previous trip to Spain and Portugal, I continued on to Scotland for a few days stay at Kingsbarns Golf Links near St. Andrews. One of Scotland's newest venues, Kingsbarns had just recently joined the Top 100 list. To complete the playing of all of the Top 100 Courses of Scotland I would have to play the list's new addition. Designed by California-based architect Kyle Phillips, the course rests near the North Sea, making it a links-style course. Every hole you play has a view of the ocean. In that sense, it truly is a sight to behold. Come the near future, I wouldn't be surprised to see a major event played there.

A few days later, I got in more rounds at my home course in Scotland, Loch Lomond Golf Club. After that, it was time to head home again. I wasn't really sure what was going to happen next though I knew a lot of golf was still left in the season. In fact, there was a ton of golf to come.

It was only a few weeks after arriving home from Scotland that I continued marching forward. I received a phone call from a friend and fellow volunteer at UCLA who told me he could set me up with a round at Valley Club of Montecito outside Santa Barbara, which is about a six-hour drive from my home in the Bay Area. Designed by Dr. Alister MacKenzie, the course provided me with an opportunity I couldn't pass up. The temperature in Santa Barbara the day of my round hovered around 90 degrees with very heavy smoke in the air from a number of nearby forest fires. Carrying my own bag made me feel like it was 100 degrees. After the round, I noticed that my feet felt numb and at times I felt a bit dizzy. Exhausted, I stopped on my way back to spend the night at a roadside hotel rather than drive home as I had planned. Maybe it was just fatigue.

Awaking the next day to complete my drive home, I still felt the sensation in my feet, as if my feet were asleep. Somehow I made the drive safely, but I knew it was time to have the situation checked out. After a visit with my personal physician, I was referred to a neurologist who determined that I was suffering from peripheral neuropathy, an incurable affliction that causes the slow deterioration of the nervous system in one's feet and legs and that can also affect certain messages to the brain. It wasn't good news, but I knew things could always be worse. The only questions I had were: How would it affect my golf game and how would it affect my travel? I still had much to do if I were to complete my quest. I had already begun planning for a September trip back to Europe, an October trip back to the East Coast and the South, and a visit to the Los Angeles basin. What would happen?

After I rested for a few months, September arrived and I was off to Europe to attend the Ryder Cup that had previously been postponed because of September 11. Before heading to the championship, I made a pit stop in Paris where I planned to play the ultra-private Morfontaine Golf Club, which is located on the northern outskirts of Paris. Jean Claude Benoist-Lucy, whom I had met during my stay in Long Island, was to be my host. Unfortunately, he couldn't play because of recent back surgery. Instead, a friend of Jean's came and picked me up at my hotel, and we played together. After arriving at the course, I was glad that I was with someone who knew where he was going.

Located in the countryside, the course is somewhat hidden. As we kept driving, I kept wondering where a golf course would be. It just didn't seem to fit the area.

Suddenly, we arrived at a simple gate with a buzzer. Inside the gate were cabins and a beautiful clubhouse, which was very secluded. Playing golf was like playing a round amid the Black Forest. I remember the club manager was so proud that their small, quaint club was ranked.

After playing golf, I thanked my host and headed to the airport for a quick flight to London where I rented a car and drove on to Birmingham for the next day's opening rounds of the Ryder Cup at The Belfry. When I originally purchased my ticket for the event, I was offered a bonus package that included admission to an opening-night gala. The evening of my arrival, I put on my tuxedo and headed to the gala. It was fabulous! The event consisted of a dinner that was attended by the American and European teams, their caddies, and their captains. Amid the celebration, various players stepped up to the podium to address the attendees. In addition, the entertainment included Ireland's famous River Dancers. I will never forget that gala. Unfortunately, that evening would be the only highlight for the Americans. By the end of the event, the Euros had won again, this time outscoring the Yanks by three points. It was the Europeans' third win in the last four championships.

Though I was disgruntled by the American loss, it wouldn't take long for my spirits to rise again.

Following the Ryder Cup, I headed to Glasgow and my European home course, Loch Lomond Golf Club. Waiting there for me were two old friends from the States, Duncan King and Mike Scofield. I had known the two since our kindergarten days in Palo Alto, a stretch of nearly 60 years. On and off the course, we had a ball. We had plenty of reminiscing mixed in with golf, fabulous meals and a few samples of 20-year-old Scotch whisky. My time with Duncan and Mike was a great way to end my latest venture across the Atlantic.

It was early fall when I returned home and made plans for my return trip to the East Coast and the South. I was again on my way, my goal being to play five more of the Top 100 courses.

Instead of starting in the South this time, I began my trip in the North with a round at Winged Foot Golf Club (East Course). A year earlier I was able to get in a round on the West Course, but I didn't have time to play the East Course. Thankfully, my gracious host Kenneth Gestal had given me another opportunity. Like the West Course, which went on to host the 2006 U.S. Open, the East Course could also swallow your scorecard. Even with a shaky score, however, I still walked away with a smile. There's just something about Winged Foot, be it the tradition, the venue, whatever. I could shoot 150 on the courses at Winged Foot and still be thrilled.

Next I was off to Nantucket Island to play at Nantucket Golf Club, which—though ranked when I played it—failed to make the 2003-2005 Top 100 list. There I was to be hosted by Walter Forbes whom I had met at a dinner in 2000 at the Greywalls Hotel in Scotland on the grounds of Muirfield. I was told to show up at the White Plains Airport where I was to board my host's private jet, which would take me to Nantucket. The passengers included my host, 20 or so of his friends and employees, and me. The jet was full. By the time we all finished a light breakfast, we were on the ground again and on our way to Nantucket Golf Club, where we all got in rounds of golf. After playing, we had lunch and were back on the jet—this time enjoying snacks and chilled white wine as we headed back to White Plains. What a way to spend a day!

Afterwards, *sans* my own personal jet, I was back in my rental car headed to Long Island for my next day's slated round at Garden City Golf Club. You'll recall that I had originally been scheduled to play Garden City in the fall of 2001, but September 11 had changed everything. Again, my host had graciously offered me the chance to return. Founded in 1898, Garden City is a par 73 with only three par-three holes. If you don't have your driver working, it can be a long day. Fortunately for me, my driver cooperated.

The next morning I flew to Atlanta to meet my friend Jim Stark. Jim had been my host at Baltusrol a year earlier and had become very instrumental in helping me gain access to some of the Top 100 courses. In Atlanta we played East Lake Golf Club, the home course of legend Bobby Jones. Only a day after our round, players were expected to start arriving for that year's PGA Championship, thus the course was in pristine condition. The back tees were closed, but the course was still demanding.

The only thing that saved my score was that the pins were in relatively easy spots to further protect the greens.

The next day, Jim and I met another one of his friends who was a member at Peachtree Golf Club. Founded in 1947, and designed by Robert Trent Jones Sr. and Bobby Jones, Peachtree is one of those venues that make you feel like royalty. When you enter, you see no signs. Then you suddenly see the clubhouse, a quaint building that served as General Sherman's home during the Civil War. Once you are on the grounds, you see that everything is immaculate. Amazingly, during our round we were one of only two foursomes on the entire course. Because the course is full of water hazards you have to be very accurate. One of the best water holes was the par-three 4th, which featured a tee shot over water to a tiny green. Later in the dining room, the number of members and guests was again small. It was a wonderful way to wrap up my trip.

On the flight home, I sat next to a very nice couple who were going from Atlanta to Chicago to attend a horse-racing event. During our conversation, I noticed that the gentleman was wearing a shirt with a golf logo on it. Of course, I struck up a conversation about golf and we were soon chatting about my quest as well as his golf interests. He told me that he annually played a round at Pebble Beach each February for his birthday. I got his name, which was Gerald Davidson, and told him that next time he was ready to play Pebble Beach to give me a ring. We never did join up for golf, but during the next two years in the month of February, I did visit him on the course while out walking with my dogs.

Speaking of phone calls, when I arrived home, I had a message from my golfing buddy who serves with me on the board at UCLA. He was wondering if I had time that December to get in a round at Riviera Country Club after the campus meetings. Knowing that the course was on my list, I quickly phoned him back and told him I'd be delighted to join him. Home of the annual Los Angeles Open, Riviera was once the stomping grounds of legend Ben Hogan. The hole that really stood out to me at Riviera was the par-three 6th, which is famous for having of all things a bunker smack dab in the middle of the green.

Overall, it had been a great year. More and more, it appeared that I would fulfill my quest.

10

The Heartland

Both in 2001 and 2002, my plan had been to concentrate as much as I could on checking off courses in the States. The key, of course, was networking. I knew that in some cases, if I didn't jump at the opportunity, it could possibly disappear. I was also beginning to feel the pressure of my timeline. If I were to complete my quest within the next two years, I would still have to play a lot of golf.

In 2003 my plan included two more fall trips, one to the Midwest and New England, the other to the Mid-Atlantic states and west stretching to the Rocky Mountain states. Overall, if things worked out I could possibly knock out 16 or so ranked courses. It would be yet another huge step in the completion of my quest.

In kicking things off, I recalled that in late 2002, my new friend Jim Stark introduced me to his old-time golfing buddy Mike Coyle. Mike, a true 2-handicap player, lived in the Chicago area and mentioned that he and some of his friends could possibly get me onto some of the ranked courses in that region. In a short matter of time, he was successful in getting me onto the top four courses in Chicago. The only course that was not ranked, Olympia Fields, oddly was the site of that year's U.S. Open.

The group of courses gave me a basis to plan the rest of my trip. Along with the Chicago golf, I would look to play nine other courses in five states in an 11-day period, starting with Crystal Downs in northern Michigan on the shores of Lake Michigan.

Two weeks before my planned departure, my host for Crystal Downs called and told me that he would not be able to meet me for personal reasons. I completely understood, but was suddenly in a pickle. Playing Crystal Downs was an integral part of my plans.

Like my earlier dilemma with Seminole in Florida, I started thinking of anyone and everyone that I had ever known from Michigan. This time, the bell rang when I remembered that my friend Jim Young had lived in Michigan, had graduated from the University of Michigan, lived and died Michigan football, and was a true "Big Blue." I decided to call him immediately.

After I explained my quest and my dilemma, he told me, "You're not going to believe this, Leon, but my wife Gail and I visited the course just a week ago. We were near the course to visit my brother who has a vacation home in the area. He doesn't play golf, but I can call him and he might know a member or someone who does." I replied, "That would certainly be appreciated" and told him the specific dates I was hoping for.

Less than 48 hours later, he called me back and said that his brother's next-door neighbor was a member and that my dates looked good with one condition: the Saturday before my dates Michigan was to play Notre Dame in Ann Arbor. Whether or not the Big Blue won or lost would influence the date of play. I called the member and set up a planned day. When Michigan won the game, I was on my way, my original plan again intact.

A few days later, I landed in Chicago, grabbed a rental car, and began the six-hour drive north around Lake Michigan to Frankfort and Crystal Downs Country Club. Opened in 1929, and designed in part by Dr. Alister MacKenzie and Perry Maxwell, Crystal Downs is an architectural masterpiece amid an unforgettably beautiful setting. Turned out, my member-host and his two fraternity brothers who joined us were Phi Gamma Deltas, the same fraternity that I had been a member of while in college. We had a lot of laughs over that. Perge!

The following day was a long one. Because I missed the early morning ferry that crosses Lake Michigan from upstate Michigan to Wisconsin, I had to drive nine hours back through Chicago where I then turned north and headed to Whistling Straits Golf Course in Kohler, just north of Milwaukee. What made the trip so exhausting was the hot September weather and its humidity, which is especially hard on a Californian. What was equally difficult was the toll road system. It seemed that about once every ten minutes, I was scrounging in my pockets for another 40 cents. The trip, however, was definitely worth it. One of architect Pete Dye's latest creations, Whistling Straits is gorgeous. It was like I was playing golf in a national park.

A bit behind in time, I unfortunately couldn't stay long. After a quick meal, I was back in the car headed again to Chicago where I was to meet two friends for rounds at four of the top courses in the Windy City area. My Chicago experience began with a round at

One Man's Opinion
Most Overstated Entrance Medinah *Like visiting a shrine*
Most Overstated Clubhouse Medinah *A bit too massive*
Most Understated Entrance The Honors *Very simple with no signs*
Most Mountainous Course Wade Hampton *Fazio's first course*
Worst Weather Fishers Island *Tail end of Hurricane Isabel 2003*

Medinah Country Club, where I played the No.3 course. Carved out of a forest, Medinah No.3 had previously hosted three U.S. Open championships (1949, 1975, and 1990). In the summer of 2006, the course hosted the PGA Championship. Overall, Medinah's setting is one of grandeur. From the entrance to the clubhouse, you feel as if you're entering some sort of shrine, which you are.

A day later, it was a round at the Chicago Golf Club. Another one of America's oldest courses, Chicago was founded in 1895. In the early 1900s, it

One Man's Opinion

Most Difficult Course
Pine Valley
Just a plain brute

Worst Score
Pine Valley
90 gross, again a brute

Best Dish
Snapper Turtle Soup,
Pine Valley
Simply delicious

Best Grill
Pine Valley
Tradition and atmosphere

hosted multiple U.S. Opens. Indeed, it is a classic. At both venues, our member-hosts were extremely gracious and welcoming, much more so than the courses, as my scores testified.

On day three of my Chicago whirlwind, we played unranked Olympia Fields Country Club, which earlier had hosted the U.S. Open won by Jim Furyk. On day four, the final day of our Chicago venture, we played Shoreacres Golf Course on the rim of Lake Michigan. Our scheduled day at Shoreacres was a Monday, when most private courses are closed. In this case, the superintendent made an exception and opened the course and provided us with a caddie. We had the course all to ourselves. Like Whistling Straits, the course was full of birds and wildlife. It truly was like a walk in the park. The only background noise other than birds chirping was some music being played at the nearby Great Lakes Naval Training Center for the morning's drill sessions.

After the round, my golfing buddies and I parted. For me, it was time to again march on, this time my destination being a night flight to Boston for an early morning's drive the next day south to New London, where a ferry would take me across Long

Island Sound to Fishers Island Golf Club. The day of my round, the course was being hit by the tail end of Hurricane Isabel. I loved it. For me, it was like playing a round in Scotland or Ireland. During play, the winds gusted up to 60 mph and nearly three inches of rain fell. My host, a younger fellow named Clayson Davis, kept looking at me throughout the round and asking if I'd had enough golf for the day because of the weather. "Hell no," I replied. "I rather enjoy the walk." Deep down, I knew I was in part lying to myself. The weather was atrocious, yet I wasn't going to be the first one to wave the white flag. Besides, I knew that it was perhaps the only chance I'd ever get to play the course. Being on my list of Top 100 courses, Fishers Island was a course I had to finish. Clayson and the other members of my foursome must have thought I was completely loony.

After drying off and warming up, I returned to the ferry for the short ride to New London, where I then drove through the bad weather to Boston for my next day's planned round at The Country Club in Brookline. I was exhausted from the previous day, but I managed to meet my host at the starter's shack. My host and I were paired with another two-some and off we went for what would turn out to be an excellent round of golf. The previous day's storm had passed, and the weather was crystal clear. The three other players in my group were fine golfers, and their play rubbed off on me. In golf, I think it's true that on most occasions you play to the level of the people you're playing with. Play with high-handicappers, and your score will rise. Play with low-handicappers, and your score will drop. Along with the golf, what was great for me at The Country Club was remembering the Ryder Cup that had been played on the course in 2000. I had watched the event and was now walking the same fairways. In my quest, the highlights were playing the courses where I had seen history unfold. Already many courses that I had played had hosted a U.S. Open, British Open, or PGA Championship. There were more to go.

After an eight-hour drive through horrible weather from Boston, following a five-hour round of golf, I eventually arrived in Rochester, New York for my next morning's round at Oak Hill Country Club. One of Donald Ross's creations, the East Course at Oak Hill only months earlier had hosted the 2003 PGA Championship won by upstart Shaun Micheel. As I expected, the course and the clubhouse dripped history even though Xerox's morning news of large layoffs dimmed the clubhouse lunch conversation.

Everything had been great. It was time to head home. Little did I know what was waiting for me.

The next morning, I headed back home following a quick layover in Chicago. After landing at O'Hare Airport, I was walking off the plane to change flights when my arm suddenly caught a sharp, jagged strip of metal torn from the jetway wall. I began bleeding profusely and responded by covering my arm with my coat. As I entered the airport concourse, I made a beeline for the men's room where I wrapped my gash in a handful of wet paper towels. I then proceeded to the nearest airline check-in area to tell the clerks what had happened and that I needed medical attention before I hopped on my soon-to-depart flight to San Francisco. At the desk, the airline employee was a bit baffled by what had happened and told me that I had to fill out an accident report before doing anything. Still bleeding, I left for a return trip to the men's room for more makeshift bandages. I didn't have time for paperwork. I had to find the first aid station fast.

After passing about what seemed to be a parade of Starbucks coffee stands, I finally found the first aid area. It seemed the only person there was a doctor. I knocked on the door and rang the buzzer numerous times before he finally emerged. He told me I would have to wait at least an hour because he was currently treating someone who had overdosed on drugs. I explained to the doctor that I couldn't wait that long because my flight was to leave in an hour or so. I further told him that I would fix myself if shown where the gauze, tape, and cold water was. He agreed that it was okay and showed me the goods that I needed. I mended myself as best I could, made it to my flight, and was headed home for a much-needed break. Of course, my rest would last only a little more than a month.

Not long after returning home, I recalled that my member-host at Pine Valley Golf Club in New Jersey had told me that I was set for a rain-check date at his course. The previous Memorial Day weekend I had been scheduled to play the course, but bad weather hit. I waited two days in a hotel at the Philadelphia Airport, but the weather never cleared. The new offer was just what I was wishing for. I began to complete my plans for yet another trip, starting in the East and moving towards the West. The trip would ultimately involve nine of the Top 100 courses, located across eight states. I would try to make it all happen in only a span of 12 days including cross-country flights. It would include over 7,000 miles in the air and 2,400 miles in a rental car. Though my arm had healed, it was still a daunting idea, but I had to do it. It was part of my quest!

In the latter days of the fall, I was indeed back at it. My first leg was a flight from San Francisco to Newark, New Jersey, where I would begin my next trek at Somerset Hills Country Club. From there, I would head south before turning around and heading west towards Denver.

I arrived in Newark in the evening, which made things a bit difficult for me. I don't know how the locals feel, but the signs on the New Jersey highways to me are barely legible at night. Very little light shines on them. As a result, I continually had to pull over onto the shoulder and stop to read the signs. I got completely turned around at one point. My 20-minute drive to Bernardsville, where I was to lodge for the night, turned out to be an hour long.

Early the next morning, I met my member-host John Grymes for play at Somerset Hills, an A.W. Tillinghast design that first opened in 1917. John was extremely excited that day. Earlier he had heard the good news that he had become a new member at nearby Pine Valley and his 11-year-old son had just carded his first-ever hole-in-one.

After the round, John mentioned to me that the United States Golf Association headquarters was just a short distance away in Far Hills and that if I had time, I should stop by. Because it was on my way to Pine Valley, where I was slated to play the following day, I did indeed stop by the USGA. If you're an avid golfer or simply a fan of the game, I highly recommend a visit. Amid beautiful grounds is a wonderful golf museum, a gift shop and the laboratories where the USGA conducts its research on agronomy and golf equipment.

That evening, I had dinner with my Pine Valley member-host Scott Smith. Joining us were Scott's wife and two of his friends who were to be a part of our foursome for Pine Valley. As usual, the subject of my quest was brought up with the normal questions: "So, how many courses have you completed? Which ones? Which ones remain? What's been your favorite?" In a discussion of the courses I had yet to play, South Africa-based Durban Country Club always drew the most attention. Someone would always ask, "How are you going to find a member of a course that far away?" As luck would have it, Scott's friends—the Hansens—had played Durban before and knew a member quite well. They gave me his phone number and told me to give him a ring when I was ready to go. What an amazing coincidence!

The next day, while driving to the course I began to wonder what was waiting for me. I was going to Pine Valley Golf Club, which is considered the top golf course in the world and the most difficult. Along the way, we passed through some small residential areas, a run-down amusement park, and a railroad line. Then, all of a sudden, a small sign pointed to Pine Valley Golf Club. Once through a security gate, you are free to enjoy the 700 acres of forest that surround the course. The facilities are as grand as one would expect, complete with cabins, a few private houses, and a clubhouse that couldn't be any more traditional. There's a saying at Pine Valley that the caddies will bet if you haven't played the course before, you will not score less than ten strokes over your handicap index. They couldn't be more correct and then may even be conservative.

The course, which features the touch of many of golf's greatest architects, is long and tough with huge carry areas. It has also only one set of tees. One's physical capabilities and mental capacity are tested throughout all 18 holes, with no time to take a deep breath. My favorite Pine Valley story is that of amateur Woody Platt. During a round one day, Platt started with a birdie at No.1, an eagle at No.2, a hole-in-one at No.3, and yet another birdie at No.4. He was 6-under through the first four holes. Platt, in a great mood, went to the clubhouse for a quick celebration, which lasted a long time. He never returned to finish his round.

Following my fabulous experience at Pine Valley, I thanked my member-host and headed south towards Bethesda, Maryland, in preparation for my next day's round at Congressional Country Club, home to two fine courses.

My member-host, her son, and I played the Blue

Course at Congressional. The tradition of the course rests in its history, beginning with the club's first president, President Woodrow Wilson, and continues today with its heavy influence of top government officials from nearby Washington D.C. As we played, a group of three presidential helicopters flew overhead on their way from the capital to Camp David. I was told they always travel in threes—the president in one—to deter identity in case of an attack or threat. Also, while playing the 15th hole, I was told about a huge house that bordered the fairway that was once owned by professional boxer Mike Tyson. Apparently, when he owned the home his security guards would patrol the perimeter with leashed tigers. Unbelievable!

The following morning, another beautiful day, I had a day of driving the car instead of my ball. I had a seven-hour drive south on Interstate 75 to southern Virginia for a short stay at the Homestead Resort in Hot Springs, home of legend Sam Snead. As I discovered, to fully experience the Homestead (Cascades Course), one must also stay at the grand old Homestead Hotel and have dinner at Sam Snead's Tavern across the street. The tavern is full of Snead memorabilia, and the waitresses are full of stories about the legendary golfer, who at the time of my visit had just recently passed away.

After dinner, I went straight to bed because the next day I faced another long drive, this time to Chattanooga, Tennessee, on the border of Georgia and Arkansas. After more sleep and a drive the next day, I played The Honors Course, a new course designed by Pete Dye and developed by Coca-Cola magnate Jack Lupton. At The Honors course, the focus is purely on amateur golf, not professional. Not soon after opening, it hosted the 1991 U.S. Amateur championship. My foursome included two Brits who were members of Formby Golf Club near Southport in northwest England, a course that I had played five years earlier. During our round, we chatted quite a bit about the courses in England.

Another day came, and I was in the car yet again on a long trip, keeping up with the demanding schedule. I was now headed back east a bit through the southern portion of the Great Smoky Mountains and the Cherokee National Forest. By now, I was tired of sitting in the car, but this drive was gorgeous. In late fall, the leaves had turned golden with tints of red and orange. The leaves, the streams, and rivers created a photographer's paradise. I could only imagine how someone like Ansel Adams would have felt. After winding through the forest, I went 4,500 feet up in elevation, which eventually landed me in Cashiers, North Carolina, where I was to play Wade Hampton Golf Course. Playing there was my first-ever round on a mountain course. It was spectacular. At times, it was hard to focus on the golf. The scenery itself was simply breathtaking.

Again on the move the next morning, I drove southwest to Atlanta where I was to board a short flight to Tulsa, Oklahoma. I was slowly heading back home, but I still had three courses to play. At the time of my arrival in Oklahoma, the Sooners football team was ranked No.1 in the country. Everywhere you looked were red and white signs proclaiming "We're No.1" and "Go Sooners." In Tulsa, I got in a round at Southern Hills Country Club, which in 2001 had hosted the U.S. Open won by South African Retief Goosen. As I had seen during the Open, the course was tight. That's exactly how it played. Accuracy was at a premium.

Following my round at Southern Hills, I drove the next day north to Hutchinson, Kansas, for another round of golf Midwest-style at Prairie Dunes Country Club. I couldn't believe that a Top 100 golf course could be located in the heart of wheat and oil country. Yet there it was. Ironically, the course and Kansas would instantly gain a place in my heart. To start things off, I was paired with a member and one of the club's assistant pros. Both were very fine golfers and knew the course inside and out. They helped me around tremendously. As for the course, I realized that you didn't have to be on the coast or in the mountains or forest to enjoy spectacular golf scenery. While Prairie Dunes was somewhat simple in its design, sitting in a wheat field, its architect Perry Maxwell certainly made it a great test of golf. It was like the movie *Field of Dreams* but instead was Course of Dreams. That evening, I stayed in Hutchinson. I had played eight courses in ten days, having covered ten states and over 7,000 miles.

The night of my stay, I asked some of the locals for a place where I could go for a traditional type of supper. After a fine meal, with the outside temperature at 85 degrees, I decided that I would sit on a bench near the restaurant and rest. The sky was crystal clear and full of stars. In the background, crickets sang their ode to the night. The air was full of the smell of freshly cut wheat, fantastic if you understand. Suddenly, in the background a lonesome whistle of a freight train blew in the distance. I was in the Heartland. I sat on that bench for over an hour, sitting back and soaking it all in. The only thing missing was Cathy to enjoy my experience.

After Kansas, I was off to Denver for a slated round at Cherry Hills. The forecast called for temperatures in the low 40s and snow flurries. Because it was my last stop, I marched on, hopping onto Interstate 70 for what turned out to be about an eight-hour drive through at times extremely heavy prairie winds. The only amusing break I got during the drive was that at one point, a line of over 30 cars and trucks passed me by, all adorned in red and white with University of Oklahoma flags or signs. They were those rabid Sooners fans again, headed to Boulder, Colorado, for Saturday's game against the University of Colorado. Fans all vary in their style of rooting depending on their geographic location.

As for Denver, it's one of my favorite cities. I had spent a lot of time in the area in recent years and always had a marvelous experience. This time, I was there to play Cherry Hills Country Club. I had first been to Cherry Hills as a youngster in 1954, while on a football recruiting trip to the University of Colorado. Even though I wasn't interested in golf at the time, my alumni recruiter Jack Fuller was a member of Cherry Hills and he showed me the club.

Coming from a blue-collar background, I was thrilled to see the inside of a private country club, which I had never seen before. I'll never forget, during our visit we were having lunch when Jack whispered to me, "Do you recognize that man over there?" It was then-President Dwight D. Eisenhower. An avid golfer, he came to Cherry Hills quite often while his wife Mamie visited her mother in Denver.

When I first met my host and son at the clubhouse the day of my round, he took me on a tour of the facility. During the tour, I mentioned my previous visit. He directed me to the club's Eisenhower Room, which is dedicated to him. Among the items on display was a bust of Ike that once stood in the Oval Office.

Later, we enjoyed yet another great round of golf. Somehow, we managed to get a break in the weather. The very next day of my scheduled flight back home, snow flurries hit the area. I'd made it out just in time. Nine courses, eight states, 12 days, 7,000 miles of air time, and 2,400 miles of Hertz rental car time. Every course on my planned list for the year was checked off. My quest was suddenly nearing completion.

CHAPTER

11

The Long Haul

When I arrived back in the Bay Area in the latter portion of 2003, I was exhausted. Soon, though, I would be exhilarated. During my latest trip across the States, Cathy had started participating in a very concentrated fear-of-flying program that involved virtual reality. Just a few months later in early January, she surprised me by presenting two tickets for a short trip to Cabo San Lucas, Mexico. When I asked who they were for, she replied they were for the two of us. I was thrilled! Cathy would again be at my side!

Off we went on a fabulous three-day vacation, in part because we got in a round at Cabo del Sol Golf Course, a Jack Nicklaus signature course located on the oceanfront. It was a great way to kick off the New Year.

I had hoped that 2004 would be the year that I wrapped up my quest, but after re-examining the

2003 list of the Top 100 courses, I found that I had lost four courses that I'd played and instead gained four new ones. I realized that I had to complete the list before the fall of 2005; otherwise, I could find myself again losing and gaining venues, which was a huge challenge in my quest. With the list changing every two years, I had to adapt. If a course was dropped, it didn't count in my quest. If a course was added, I had to play it no matter where it was in the world.

With the latest changes in my mind, I began to focus on past networking and getting in the courses that I thought I could get onto as quickly as possible. The course that immediately came to my mind was Durban Country Club in South Africa. Getting on was one thing. Getting there was another. It involved a long flight to London, followed by another long flight to South Africa. I remembered my connection with the Harrises from Minneapolis during my trip to Pine Valley, and began making plans. Knowing that I would have to change flights in Europe, I began rechecking my list to see if anything new had popped up. Indeed, the European Golf Club just south of Dublin had been added, and El Saler Golf Club in Spain remained unplayed because of a rainout a few years earlier. I would start in Spain, head north to Ireland and Scotland, and then fly to South Africa. Overall, the trip would involve four courses and 13 flights spanning 28,000 miles, all to be done in 17 days.

My first destination was El Saler Golf Club on the coast of the Mediterranean Sea in Spain. Because it is a resort course, I didn't need a member-host. Originally, I had wanted to play the course during a trip to Europe in 2001, but I was rained out. Interestingly, El Saler looked like an American golf course but played like a European links. Surely not a Top 100 course, but it was on the list.

After playing El Saler, I flew back to London and then to Dublin to play the European Golf Club. A newcomer to the list, European Golf Club is again a private but publicly accessible course, making a member-host unnecessary. A newer course designed by Pat Ruddy, European Golf Club rests right alongside the Irish Sea, providing a wonderful links experience and terrific winds.

After my round there, I hopped on a quick flight to Glasgow, Scotland, where I would stay and play at Loch Lomond. Since I had become a member, Loch Lomond's reputation had grown rapidly.

After a few days at Loch Lomond, however, I was to embark on my longest trek yet. I was set for my lengthy flight from London to Durban, South Africa, where I was to tackle Durban Country Club.

Before my leaving, my host-to-be John Terry-Lloyd had sent me an e-mail telling me "Your two-day visit will be an experience you shant ever forget." After a 12-hour flight straight down the middle of Africa, I landed in Johannesburg where I then left on a short flight for Durban. When I met John, he indeed had mapped out an exciting 48-hour trip. I was first driven to my hotel, a five-star facility on the beach, where we reviewed his itinerary. The weather couldn't have been more perfect. Originally, I had planned two days in case of bad weather. With the sun out, I basically had an extra day so the next morning we drove about three hours west along the Indian Ocean to a newer course, Wild Coast Sun Golf Club.

Wild Coast is part of a rather large casino complex that at one time boomed. In recent years, however, the gaming laws had changed, and now the casino is a bit run-down. Nevertheless, the course for us was in fine shape. Because of the hilly terrain and distances between tees and greens, golf carts were recommended. Along with having to use a cart, John and I also had to have a forecaddie. Our forecaddie was a native African woman named Shela. Shela was very heavy-set and strong-looking, wore a red dress and bandana, simple rubber-type sandals, and carried a snake stick. In the surrounding four-foot-high elephant grass that is the deep rough, at times the deadly black and green mamba snakes lurk. Oh great, I thought. Yet again more snakes. I managed to hit

One Man's Opinion
Slowest Play
Cabo del Sol
Resort golf
Best Yardage Book
Cabo del Sol
Cleverly done
Best Food at the Turn
Cabo del Sol
Three free tacos
Most Overrated Course
El Saler
Two good holes and that's it
Best Wildlife
Durban
Monkeys and snakes
Worst Finishing Hole
No.18, Durban
250-yard, par-four
Longest Trip for One Round
Durban
26,000 miles

only one ball in that heavy rough, and when Shela took out her stick to look for my ball, I simply gestured to her to leave it alone. She didn't speak English, but did know a few terms from her forecaddie work such as "nice shot, good putt and be on." When you hit a nice shot, she would also applaud.

At the completion of play, I gave her a tip equivalent to ten American dollars, which was a large sum for her. Upon receiving her tip, she hugged me, smiled, kissed the money, and walked away. Oftentimes, Americans take a lot for granted. Shela had no car, no bike nor bus to take, and I was told she walks eight miles in her rubber sandals to the course every day, each way.

John and I then returned to the clubhouse to wash up before having a bite to eat and driving home. As we later approached our car, a slew of monkeys invaded the parking lot. I was completely shocked. John told me, "Just wait until tomorrow at Durban. They're everywhere."

The next day John again picked me up at my hotel to take us to Durban Country Club for our scheduled round. When we arrived, a local newspaper reporter was there to greet us. Apparently, John had told the local press about my quest. The reporter snapped off a few photos and interviewed me about my golf journey. It was quite a surprise.

After the interview was over, we teed off. Even though it was a bit late in the day it was still rather warm. As John said, monkeys were all over the course. They didn't bother you, but rather just stared at you constantly wherever you were on the course. It was almost like having a gallery. At one point, we counted a throng of 13 monkeys in one pack. Another time, I was about to tee off when there was a huge thump in the background. Apparently a rather large monkey had dove for a bird's nest, missed, and hit the deck. As we wrapped up the round, darkness was approaching. Lined up behind the green on the 18th were a number of John's friends, rooting us on. Afterwards, we all shared laughs and tales over a frosty beer.

As I was leaving the next day, I realized what a great time I'd had. Golf was my primary reason for visiting South Africa, but I had many other reasons to be happy. I met some wonderful people and learned a lot about apartheid, the astounding rate of AIDS, the increasing crime rate, and other national issues. These were people who dealt with those issues every day of their lives. While I was there, I purchased a book entitled *A Shackled Continent,* which says it all.

When I returned home, I e-mailed a thank-you letter to John.

"Dear John....Just thought I would say hello and congratulate you on the South African team's gold medal in the swimming relays in Athens. I have read about the recent political party consolidations and hope it is a positive step for your country. I often think about my fantastic experience in SA: Your hospitality, Shela and the monkeys. Thank you, thank the head pro, and thank your wife and friends. Hit 'em straight, enjoy life and I'll see you in the summer of 2005.
Regards, Leon."

CHAPTER

CHAPTER

12

Staying in the States

W hile I had a wonderful time in South Africa, when I got back home, I felt a sense of relief. I had checked off what appeared to be one of my biggest challenges, that being to play Durban Country Club. Still, however, I had a ways to go to complete my quest. For starters, I thought it would be appropriate to continue making my way across America because plenty of courses were left in the States to play. When I sat down to make plans for the summer of 2004, I originally thought I'd need about three contacts. Turned out, I needed 17 contacts to wrap up what would be a six-course trip covering three states.

My return journey across America began in Baltimore where I met my good friend Mike Coyle and his good friend Brad Burris, who lived in North Carolina. Brad, an accomplished amateur player, knew a fellow named Peter Smith who was a member of the Baltimore Country Club. Smith had set up a date for us to join him at Baltimore Country Club (Five Farms East).

At the course, we began with a superb lunch that, of course, featured a bowl of Maryland crab soup, which was as wonderful as the famous bowl of snapper turtle soup that I had at Pine Valley. Afterwards, it was time to play. On the course, I quickly noticed that many of the trees and plants looked as if they were dried up. As Peter Smith explained, it was the result of cicadas, a locust-type critter about four inches in length that emerges only once every 17 years. Thing is, when they swarm it's "en masse." I recalled that earlier in the year during the annual Memorial Tournament in Ohio, the Muirfield course had been invaded by the little buggers, which when together produce a continuous loud and unique sound that one could hear over the television.

Following our round, we drove a short distance to spend the night and play golf the next day at Caves Valley Golf Club. Another newer Tom Fazio design, the course was not ranked at the time but was worthy. As well as being home to a great course, the venue also houses a golf academy that is one of the greatest in the country.

While at Caves Valley, Brad told me a story regarding last year's U.S. Senior Open championship at Inverness. Brad played in the same group as Arnold Palmer. During the round, Palmer ripped open the entire seat of his pants while playing a difficult bunker shot. Brad told me Palmer took it in great humor and his pants were literally mended with a series of large safety pins, all to the delight of the gallery.

After our day at Caves Valley, we began going our separate ways. While Mike and I left for the airport, Brad—a member at Caves Valley—stayed behind to play in an upcoming member-guest tournament at the club. Mike, like Brad, was also off to play in a member-guest tournament, an event in Rockford, Illinois, his hometown. I meanwhile had my quest, which meant a flight to Detroit and a drive south to Toledo, Ohio, for a round at Inverness Golf Club, the next day.

At Inverness, my member-host was a fellow named Greg Kopan. Included in my group were also a gentleman named Tom, who was a friend of Brad Burris, and another member named John Nelson, who was a young attorney. During our round, John relayed to me a rather interesting and amusing story.

The tale involved John, a newcomer to the club, once signing off for a hot dog at the turn. The charge was $2.65. A few months went by before the club sent a statement. Apparently, because John Nelson was a newer member his name wasn't recognized. Instead, the bill landed in the hands of former Inverness head pro and golfing legend Byron Nelson. Byron wrote a letter back to the club explaining that while he was indeed a member, he hadn't been to the club for over 20 years. John told me that when he heard the story, he didn't care about paying for the $2.65 hot dog. What he wanted was the letter from Byron Nelson so that he could frame it and hang it in his office. When John pursued this matter, he learned that the accounting office had destroyed the letter. Oh well.

After my round at Inverness, I was off on a three-hour drive north through intermittent rain to Bloomfield Hills north of Detroit, where I was to play Oakland Hills Country Club. Greg Slossinger, superintendent of Caves Valley, had arranged a round for me on Oakland Hills South Course.

Arriving at the club, I was met by my member-host, Jamie Dougherty. Because the 2004 Ryder Cup was to be played at Oakland Hills in only a few months, the course was in perfect shape and the members were excited. Oakland Hills officials had also just recently opened their $26 million remodeled clubhouse, which was surrounded by a beautiful array of red, white and blue flowers with a flag at half-staff in honor of President Ronald Reagan's recent passing. It was quite a sight to behold.

Following a rather difficult round, we headed to the bar area for refreshment. While there, I happened to recognize baseball hall-of-fame player Ralph Kiner and several former Detroit Tigers. Apparently they were at the course celebrating the 20th anniversary of winning the World Series. Earlier at Caves Valley, I also had the pleasure of seeing former Baltimore Orioles star Brooks Robinson. Both occasions were a thrill even for an average baseball fan.

Still, I had to keep moving on. Following a brief overnight stay, I was up early and back in the saddle for a lengthy drive that took me to Dublin, Ohio, for my next scheduled round at Muirfield Village Golf Club. Only a few days earlier, Jack Nicklaus had hosted his annual Memorial Tournament on the course. In the clubhouse, I was treated to what was basically a shrine to Nicklaus and other legends past and present. On the course, the leaderboard with all of the players' names was still up showing Vijay Singh the victor. When my host-to-be, New York resident Bruce Alonso, was unable to play, I walked the course, a fantastic but treacherous layout, by myself. My thrill at Muirfield Village was walking up the fairway of No.18 alone with the leaderboard still there. I kept thinking about how many times some of golf's greats had made the walk to the 18th green. To cap things off right, I stuck my approach onto the green, eventually two-putting for a final par. The cameras and fans weren't there, but for a split second I felt like a champion.

A day after my round at Muirfield Village was somewhat of an off day. During my planning, I had scheduled in one open day in case of bad weather. It was humid, but so far no rain had fallen. Taking advantage of my day off, I decided to visit the new Jack Nicklaus museum on the grounds of Ohio State University. If you're a Nicklaus fan or a golf fan, I highly recommend a visit. Along with being an ode to the Golden Bear, the museum is a celebration of the game of golf.

Rested up, I was back the next day to golfing, which meant a round at Scioto Country Club in Columbus, a course that has a traditional layout like a majority of Midwest courses. To meet me at Scioto was my member-host Joe Bettendorf, at the time the course's club champion. Joining us was one of Joe's friends and the club professional, J.J. Walker. Both were fine players, and at times it was tough to even think of keeping up with them. They understood, however, and tried to help me as much as possible. J.J., to me, was extremely interesting. A young up-and-comer, J.J. in a few months was to marry his longtime sweetheart and a month later he became the new co-head professional at Augusta National. Overall, it was a very pleasant day, and I even won a few holes thanks to my handicap index.

My latest Midwest/Northeast excursion was coming to an end. I had so far escaped any severe delaying weather, which is good for June in the Midwest. Next up was a day's drive to Cincinnati, and the weather again cooperated. Problem was, the next day's forecast for my final round at Camargo Club was thunderstorms.

At Camargo, my member-host-to-be Carl Linden also could not be present. Instead, I played with one of the club pros, Craig Plumber. Like all of the other pros I had played with, Craig obviously knew his game. He also knew just about everything about Camargo. During our round, Craig told me tales about the club, the area, and everything in between. By the time we were done, I felt like I had taken a tour. It was very enlightening and a great way to wrap up my latest trip. I had checked off the major-ity of courses in the States, yet North America was-n't quite finished.

Back in the cooler air of the Bay Area, I began making my plans for the fall portion of 2004. If I got to my destinations early enough, I wouldn't have to worry about snow and freezing temperatures. My first trip would be a quick hop to Canada. The second would involve a brief visit to Nebraska.

When the first week of September arrived, I was off to Canada on a six-day trip that would feature playing at the country's only two ranked courses: Highlands Links in Nova Scotia and St. George's in Toronto.

My first stop was the great old city of Halifax in Nova Scotia, which is renowned for its fishing and lumber trades. After a night's sleep, I drove six hours to the small coastal village of Ingonish, home to Highlands Links.

Regarded as Canada's finest golfing venue, Highlands Links is located within Cape Breton National Park and features both a Mountain and an Ocean Course. My immediate impression was that I was back in Scotland, which all but made sense in that Nova Scotia is Latin for New Scotland. To reinforce the Scottish feeling, the onsite lodge is the Keltic Lodge, which in the evenings features Scottish music and dancing.

Before leaving for my trip, I had seen that employees of the Canadian National Park Service were on strike, which created the possibility that the courses would be closed. I had seen this news item only a day before leaving, but I thought I would take my chances. As it was, I had few problems. The only comment I heard was from an elderly employee as I went to tee off. He had asked that I respect the picket line and not play. I replied by telling him that I understood his feelings but that I was on a quest and that I had traveled over 4,000 miles to play the course. I went on and played through a rain that quickly made the picket line disperse. Then, I was back to the Keltic Lodge for another great night that began with a lobster dinner. To my amazement, even the local McDonald's offered McLobsters, tiny nuggets of lobster instead of chicken.

The following day, I was headed straight back to Halifax where I caught a plane for a quick two-hour flight to Toronto and my next destination, St. George's Golf and Country Club.

St. George's, praised by tour players for its constant demand for accuracy and four finishing holes, has hosted several championships, including the Canadian Open four times. I found myself yet again playing in a small club tournament. Rounding out my foursome were Robert Thompson, a local newspaper golf reporter, Ian Andrew, a golf course architect who had restored the course's bunkers, and the course superintendent. As with all of my other

One Man's Opinion

Most Natural Course
Sand Hills
Includes all-natural bunkers

Most Rural Course
Sand Hills
Dead center in Nebraska

Best New Course in 25 Years
Sand Hills
A gem

Best Dish #2
Maryland Crab Soup, Baltimore
Again, simply delicious

tournament experiences, I had a marvelous time that culminated in a post-tourney celebration back at the clubhouse. Looking back, I still don't know what it was. Somehow, I always seemed to be in the right place at the right time as a guest. You never know what luck lies around the corner.

About three weeks later after a brief return home from my trip to Canada, I was off again on a weekend trip to Nebraska to play Sand Hills Golf Club.

During my previous trip through America's heartland, I had somehow missed Sand Hills. On reflection, I could see why. As I later discovered, people I had known who once lived in Nebraska had never heard of the course. They hadn't even heard of Mullen, the rural town where the course sits. Located almost dead center in the middle of Nebraska, the course features over 700-plus acres of rolling sand hills covered with prairie grasses with not a tree in sight.

In this spot, however, lies what is arguably the best-kept secret in golf. Sand Hills is an absolutely fantastic golf course. It is so wonderful that it has been compared to the Old Course at St. Andrews. Course designers Ben Crenshaw and Bill Moore have crafted an unmistakable link to the past.

The day I was there, I played my first round on foot in prairie winds that at times were gusting up to 50 mph. Later the same day, I played the course again, this time in a cart. I could have played it more. It is indeed a special place. The only thing is that because of the weather it is only open June through October. I can't wait to go back again some day.

Back home again, I thought my 2004 summer plans were done. Then, I found out that my good friend Jim Stark had called and asked about the possibility of my taking a trip back to the South for a pair of rounds at Yeamans Hall in Charleston, South Carolina, and Ocean Forest in Sea Island, Georgia. It was to be another quick trip since the courses were basically in the same geographical area.

Early that fall, I arrived in Atlanta where Jim was waiting for me. Our plan was to head straight for Charleston, but being so close to Augusta, we decided to take a short detour and drive through the town that is home to Augusta National Golf Club. We didn't have a tee-time there, but it was still interesting to see. It reminded me that at some point, I would have to figure out a way to get onto the hallowed grounds to complete my quest.

After a night's rest in Charleston, Jim and I were up early for our scheduled round at Yeamans Hall Country Club. An old Southern golf course, Yeamans Hall sits along tidelands that are home to more than a few alligators. During the round, just Jim and I were out there with an occasional gator showing up every now and then. Though I'd had my experiences with snakes, gators are obviously a different monster, another one I'd like to avoid.

We got in our round—minus any major gator meetings—and stopped by the old clubhouse for a quick bite. During our break, we met a Yeamans Hall member named Bruce Seauson. A University of Michigan grad, Bruce at the time was undergoing treatment for cancer and was looking for someone who possibly knew of a clinical trial in which he could participate. When I got home, I called colleagues of mine at the Jonsson Comprehensive Cancer Center at UCLA to see if they had a specific trial that would fit his type of cancer, and if so, how could I get the two together. I got Bruce and the center in touch with one another, but have not heard anything since.

Our next stop was Ocean Forest Golf Club in Sea Island, Georgia. We started our Ocean Forest experience with a tour of the island and all of its beautiful mansions that date back over a century. Arriving at the course, we ventured through very secluded grounds and the well-guarded main gate. One of the newest venues in the region, the course features a rather traditional front-nine. On the back, you were suddenly playing links golf. It was a fantastic venue, even though we again had to be on gator watch.

We finished up our golf with a lunch of southern shrimp chowder, after which Jim drove me back to Atlanta for my flight back home. During my quest and to this day, it's always great to see Jim. He's the epitome of a southern gentleman.

13

Pebble Beach-
Japanese Connection

During the early stages of my quest, my goal was to knock out as many overseas courses as possible. For the most part, I had met my quota. But I still had to golf in Japan, which has three of the world's Top 100 courses. For over three years, I had tried to find a source with some kind of a connection in Japan. Every time I came up empty. At one point, I had managed to secure a tee-time at one of the courses, but I still had to wait for approval from the club's board of directors. I then secured a time, but it was an inconvenient date because I needed to get all three courses in a single trip. Flying to Japan is a long haul.

Now, late September 2004, I knew I had to somehow check Japan off my list. In a year, the Top 100 list would again be subject to change. If I didn't finish my quest by then, I could be looking at further road trips that I had never planned on making.

Winter was fast approaching and the clock was ticking. Having to make something happen, I called Pebble Beach Company vice-president of golf operations RJ Harper. I had known RJ since he first arrived at Pebble Beach some 15 years earlier. Soon after we spoke, we discussed my dilemma over breakfast at The Gallery near The Lodge at Pebble Beach. A week later, RJ phoned to tell me I was set to go.

RJ explained that he had called an old friend of his in Japan named Seishi Jiromaru. Seishi had been the local representative at Pebble Beach when the course was owned by a Japanese business group. Apparently, Seishi thought that RJ would be joining me on my trip, but because of business and personal obligations, RJ declined. I would be going solo.

Over the next two months, Seishi and I e-mailed one another several times before finally agreeing on an itinerary. My request was rather simple. I needed access to Japan's top three courses, the sooner the better. While it sounded easy to me, looking back it was the toughest segment of my quest.

In early December, my final itinerary was set. Seishi had invited me to play the top four courses in Japan over a five-day period. It sounded impossible, but I had to try. It could be my only chance. Twenty years earlier, I had visited China as a guest of their Building Ministry and before that, I had been in other parts of Asia while serving in the U.S. Navy as a young man, but I had never set foot in Japan. As a result, I made a concentrated effort to learn some of the basic Japanese customs, language, and geography as quickly as possible.

During my planning for the trip, Cathy began making comments implying that she might like to join me towards the tail end of my trip. She had mentioned to me that she had once been to Tokyo some 40 years ago and recalled how she loved the city and the people. Since her fear-of-flying courses, she had joined me in Mexico. Still, I wondered if she would be up for the long flight from San Francisco to Tokyo. Just a few days before I was slated to leave, I got my answer when Cathy presented me with her own tickets. I was absolutely thrilled! Again, Cathy would be at my side!

In describing the trip, Seishi had mentioned that another fellow who was a friend of his would be joining us. The gentleman's name was Raisuke Saji. Seishi never really told me much about him. Through my research, I had decided that there were two things I had

One Man's Opinion
Best Bag Tag
Hirono
A unique gold Japanese character
Most Difficult Networking
Hirono, Naruo, Kawana
Playing Japan's Top 3 in three days

to do. One was to bring some gifts for my host and others. The other was to have some business cards printed in Japanese. In Japan, it is customary to present a small gift upon meeting certain people. My choice as a gift was a number of small crystal golf bags about 2.5 inches in length with pewter golf clubs. Only two questions concerning the gift giving were yet unanswered: Who? When?

A few days later, I was off, crossing the International Date Line and heading for Japan. I landed in Osaka, about 400 miles south of Tokyo.

After a two-hour, $125 cab ride, I was at the Osaka Ritz Carlton, my home for two nights.

At the hotel, I met a young German fellow who spoke good English and worked as part of the management team. After some brief chitchat, I asked him if he would mind joining me for dinner so that I could learn more about Japan's culture and customs. He agreed to join me and I learned that he was a golfer himself. We shared a nice dinner, and along with talking about Japan, talked about the game of golf.

With the following day being a scheduled rest and recovery day, I decided to take a long walk to explore Osaka. As lunchtime approached, I thought it would be a good idea to head to an average neighborhood to see where the locals ate. In Japan, restaurants commonly advertise not by a written menu, but by pictures displaying the featured courses. At the establishment I picked, all but a few of the menu items were very tasty. During my meal, I realized that the other guests—all of whom were Japanese—seemed to be very intrigued by my presence. I was the only Westerner in the restaurant and with my fair skin and size—I'm six feet, two inches tall—I'm sure I stood out.

After my lunch and a few nods, I went back to my hotel where I was to meet Raisuke. At about the same time, Seishi was expected to arrive on a flight from Tokyo. Receiving the call from Raisuke in my room was rather exciting. I had no idea who this person was, yet he would be part of my quest. We agreed to meet for dinner. The minute I finally met him, I knew we would quickly become friends. To help, he spoke very good English, but more importantly he was simply a great person. Earlier in his life he had graduated from a small college in Colorado. He had also worked for a while as a banker in New York City. A longtime friend of Seishi, Raisuke had also been involved with the Japanese group that at one point owned Pebble Beach. I immediately felt comfortable around him and looked forward to our excursion.

After dinner, we got some sleep in anticipation of meeting Seishi the next day. We were, upon greeting one another, slated to drive for a few hours to Naruo Golf Club. In the morning, I finally got to personally meet Seishi. After a brief exchange of pleasantries, we were on our way in a company car complete with a driver.

During the ride to Naruo, I learned about Seishi and Raisuke's relationship. Close friends since their high school days, both Raisuke and Seishi were at one time the property managers of Pebble Beach Company when it was owned by the Japanese golf resort firm Taiheiyo Club. In fact, Seishi had replaced Raisuke as the key property manager during normal corporate rotation. They had both during their tenure lived in Pebble Beach. Also, they had both at one point worked as bankers in New York City. In a nutshell, the two had basically lived almost identical lives. They had forged a bond that would never be broken.

Following our drive and the duo's story, we arrived at Naruo Golf Club, where we were greeted with perfect weather. After going through the ritual of checking in, we were greeted by the club general manager, Shigeru Taobata.

Arriving at the first tee, I thought that everything would be as it always was. Check in, maybe be assigned a caddie, and go play. I was in for a surprise.

No carts nor a caddie were waiting for us. Instead, we were met at the first tee by a woman driving what looked to me like a monster cart that traveled on an electric track. It had no seats for players. The cart, one that is used at the majority of courses in Japan, is for carrying your gear. The woman operates the cart with a TV-type remote control and acts as a combination caddie and forecaddie. The cart was very odd to me. I had never seen anything like it. It reminded of one those car rides at Disneyland. It is so interesting. Everyone would be in the fairway and all of a sudden you see the cart-like vehicle going up the pathway maybe 100 yards away. Then, it parks.

Still a bit surprised, we headed for the first tee. As it was the early winter, the course condition was exactly what I expected. The majority of the rough was a dormant dull brown color, the fairways and greens being green because of a different type of turf. There was little roll in the fairways and the greens were rather slow compared to other courses I had played. Still, it was a fun round.

After playing, we had a terrific lunch followed by a short visit with the general manager. While we chatted with the general manager, he mentioned to me that someone had recently been at the course who was also trying to play all of the world's Top 100 courses. When my host asked the date of the person's tee-time, he was told November 18 at 9 a.m. As it turned out, that person was actually me! I had set a prior tee-time but had never confirmed it. As we left, the manager presented each of us with a golf glove adorned with the Naruo logo. I later gave mine to a Japanese friend because it was right-handed and I am a lefty.

Following our visit to Naruo, we drove for an hour to Kobe for a night's stay at the Okura Hotel, a 30-story beauty that sits near the harbor. During dinner, I got to taste some fresh Kobe beef, which was simply wonderful. I also had some grilled fish and vegetables. The only things that didn't quite agree with me were the raw squid and octopus. In my opinion, eating raw squid and octopus is like eating a giant rubber band. You chew and chew and chew, and then simply swallow.

The next morning, we left rather early for a round at Hirono Golf Club. Founded in 1932, Hirono is regarded as Japan's greatest course and rightly so. The entrance, clubhouse and course are all magnificent. On-site there is also a golf museum. The host course for the 2005 Japan Open, Hirono has membership fees of around $200,000 U.S. dollars. During our round we were joined by member Shigeki Kanao, who was a friend of Seishi and Raisuke. While beautiful, the course was also treacherous. One of the toughest holes was the 550-yard par-five 15th which featured a huge drive over water and card-wrecking rough. Legend has it that Jack Nicklaus is the only player to ever reach the green in two, yet at the time he was using a "super" rubber ball. Whatever the case, I will agree. The hole is the Godzilla of Japanese golf.

Naruo and Hirono checked off our list, we next headed to the airport for a flight back to Tokyo. At the airport we were again greeted by another one of Seishi's company cars, driver and all. It gave us all time to take a breather and to chat some more. That evening, we arrived at Gotemba Golf Club, an unranked course that is the flagship course of the 28 courses of Seishi's golf resort company.

Since it was rather late, a special dining room was set up for us. Neither Seishi nor Raisuke drink alcohol, but they offered me a drink of my choice. I responded that a glass of white wine would be fine. To my amazement, when the waiter brought out the bottle, it had a Pebble Beach Resorts label. I had never seen such a thing. I asked Seishi about it, and he told me that all of the Japanese members at the club loved it, mostly because it included the words "Pebble Beach." Apparently, when Seishi's firm sold its interest in the Pebble Beach Company, they negotiated a deal that would allow the Pebble Beach name to be used on the wine bottles. According to Seishi, the deal was $1 per bottle—paid to Pebble Beach—covering 10,000 bottles a year. A good deal!

In the morning, we strolled to the Gotemba Golf Academy for what I thought was to be a brief look. Seishi had set it up so that each of us would get a two-hour lesson that revolved around using the latest in video technology. The video was amazing, although I wasn't always happy when I saw myself swinging the club in slow motion.

Following our lessons, we left on a two-hour sightseeing excursion that ultimately took us to the Kawana Hotel on the coast. As we drove through the mountain areas of Fuji-Hakone-Izu National Park and Lake Achi-No-Ko, it rained continuously. At times the rain was so heavy that more than a few times the driver pulled over to wait for a break. It was only a prelude to what we were told to expect when we reached Kawana. The storm was the remnants of a typhoon that had earlier left over 1,500 people dead or missing in the Philippines.

Despite the delays, we eventually made it to Kawana where I was shown to my room. The room had a large window and patio deck that looked directly into the incoming storm. As the night wore on, the winds got stronger and the window began rattling like crazy. I closed the drapes and the shutters thinking that if things got really bad, the glass might shatter. Soon after, the noise was so intense that I couldn't sleep. I picked up my bedding and placed it on the floor near the entry door of my room. I eventually began falling asleep when all of a sudden I was awakened by the feeling that someone or something was pushing me. I immediately jumped up and turned on the light. There couldn't be any critters that strong on the fourth floor, could there? Turned out, it was someone pushing that morning's paper under the door. Suffice to say, replaying my night's restless sleep to Seishi and

Raisuke that morning made for a real interesting breakfast—laughter and eggs.

When we arrived at Kawana Golf Course (Fuji) later that morning, the skies were clear, but the winds were still howling. The Fuji Course at Kawana is extremely hilly and has seven holes that feature a long uphill walk. Tack on the 60 mph winds, and we had quite a workout. Located on the coast, Kawana is thought of by the Japanese as their Pebble Beach Golf Links. Anything but a links course, it was still a great course, even with the wind at times blowing your ball backward.

After a brief lunch with the hotel general manager, we exchanged gifts. My time with Seishi and Raisuke had come to an end. I was sad to say goodbye. I had really enjoyed their company, and we'd had a great time. Yet they had their lives and were happy to head home.

Before Seishi and Raisuke left for Tokyo, Seishi mentioned to me that he had arranged a company car for me to use. While Seishi and Raisuke went home to Tokyo on the bullet train, I was headed back to Gotemba for more golf the following day.

The driver and I arrived at Gotemba rather late where we were greeted by the resort manager Hitoshi Koura. Koura, who was to be a part of my foursome the next day, had again set up a late dinner complete with Pebble Beach Resort chardonnay. While at Gotemba on my earlier visit, the staff had asked me what I would like to have for dinner when I returned. On sitting down, I was presented with my request: an array of steamed and grilled fish *without* the raw squid and octopus. As for my accommodations, I was given the hotel's grandest room. As I was told, it was the suite that Tiger Woods used during his visits to Gotemba. I felt like royalty!

The following morning, it was time for more golf. As Hitoshi and I sat eating our breakfast we were greeted by two young women—Camy Hosino and Natsuko Murakami—who were to be the other half of our foursome. Before their arrival, I was so impressed with the view looking out of the dining-room window that I was completely caught off guard. The view of the 18th hole was overwhelming. It looked like a Japanese travel poster. The foreground was light brown, dormant rough backed by a pond and beautifully maintained greens with stark white bunkers. Beyond the green was additional light brown rough, backed by a solid growth of manicured Japanese maple trees turning colors as well as black and red pine trees. Topping all that, there was the final icing of Mt. Fuji, 3,900 meters in elevation, showing off its snow cap. It was fabulous.

At first, I thought that both Camy and Natsuko also worked at the resort. Boy, was I wrong. As I learned, the two were professionals on the LPGA Japan Tour. With the tour on off-season, the two were helping out at the Academy and were on-hand to act as hosts for certain guests.

With magnificent Mt. Fuji in the background, we all headed for the first tee and what would be a terrific round. While Hitoshi and I played well, Camy and Natsuko showed off their skills. Time and time again, their drives sailed 250 yards straight down the middle of the fairway. Afterwards I gave each of them my gift of the crystal golf bag. There were hugs and a few tears. They were so thrilled, and so was I.

After the golf, I said my goodbyes and hopped back into Seishi's company car for a long drive back to Tokyo. As happy as I was, I was soon to be giddy. It was time to meet Cathy in Tokyo.

In Tokyo, I was relieved that I had a driver. The traffic was crazy. I never would have found my way if I had to read all those signs written in Japanese. After almost an hour of driving through the city itself, we were at The Four Seasons Hotel where I was to meet my love. I was ecstatic, and when we finally met, we shared a huge hug and kisses. Cathy was with me in of all places—Japan! I couldn't have been happier to see her.

In our room, 15 minutes later the phone rang. Cathy answered, then said, "It's for you, Leon." I was somewhat stunned. Who would be calling me in Tokyo? When I heard the voice on the other line, I knew it was Seishi. He wanted to know if my second visit to Gotemba had been satisfactory. He also was wondering what Cathy and I had planned for the next three days until it was time to leave. I relayed to Seishi that our plans revolved around sightseeing and shopping, at which he quickly offered me the continued service of his company car and driver. He also asked if we would like his assistant, a woman named Keiko Hayashino, to help us with our plans so that we could get the most out of our final 72

hours. Knowing how much the driver had already
helped, I quickly agreed. Then, Seishi asked to speak
with Cathy. He wanted to make sure everything was
fine with her. When we finally got off the phone,
Cathy and I couldn't believe Seishi's hospitality. He
was adamant that we have a trip that we would
never forget *à la* John Terry-Lloyd in South Africa.

The following day, Cathy and I went for a long
walk, which included taking in the sights. Later that
day, we hooked up with Seishi's assistant, Keiko.
Keiko had worked for Seishi at Pebble Beach, at
times doing public relations, and spoke perfect
English. Upon our meeting, she immediately presented us with ideas and a timetable since we had
only two days left on the mainland. After listening,
Cathy and I decided to make the next day a sightseeing day. Our last day, we would enjoy the surroundings of the hotel while getting ready to go
home.

That evening, Cathy and I took a cab to down-
town Tokyo where we enjoyed a fabulous dinner.
The night was perfectly clear, making the numerous
neon lights glow even brighter. We had been to
Times Square in New York. Downtown Tokyo was
Times Square times 100.

The following morning, Keiko and the driver
arrived early to take us to Yokohama, the sister city
of Tokyo. We started with a few hours of shopping,
followed by lunch in, of all things, a Chinatown dis-
trict. After lunch, we were driven to the town of
Kamakura, home of the Great Buddha statue.
Approximately 50 feet in height and cast in bronze,

the Great Buddha statue has stood for over eight centuries. During our drive, Keiko also took us to a historic Buddhist temple. Both were sights to behold. Later that evening, Cathy and I parted ways with Keiko and the driver. We were exhausted, and opted to simply enjoy a relaxing dinner at our hotel. The next day we were scheduled to fly out and we both knew that it would be a very long day.

As the morning of our departure arrived, we had to say "Sayonara" to Japan. While Cathy's stay had been much briefer than mine, she too was sad to leave. In just our few days together, we had a great time. Our doorman provided a perfect send-off. As my luggage was being brought out of the hotel, he noticed that I had a traveling golf bag. He quickly told me how much he loved golf but that it was difficult for him to play because of the high costs and course accessibility. My mind quickly spinning, I remembered that I still had one crystal golf bag left in my luggage. I dug it out and presented it to him. What a reaction! As he received it, he bowed, thanked me, and began weeping.

Back at home, I couldn't stop thinking about what an incredible experience we had in Japan. Cathy was there, and during my stay, I had met Seishi and Raisuke. The golf was great, but there was something more. It was life and it was beautiful.

My Japan experience nearly made me want my quest to continue forever, yet it was coming to an end.

14

On to the Final Putt

By the time January 2005 arrived, my quest was nearly over. I had only two remaining courses, Kauri Cliffs in New Zealand and Augusta National. Looking back, I felt fortunate. During the previous years, I had experienced some wonderful moments and met a slew of beautiful people. At times, Cathy would ask me if I would ever do it again and I always replied 'Absolutely. Yes.'

Kauri Cliffs and Augusta National were my final two courses for good reason. In the case of Kauri Cliffs, during my previous visit to Australia and New Zealand, the course was not ranked. It meant another 13-hour flight to play a single course, but it had to be done if I were to complete my quest on time. As for Augusta National, I knew it would be extremely tough to gain access. Also, a part of me felt it would be fitting to start at Pebble Beach and finish at Augusta National. In a sense, it was like having two great bookends.

Still recovering a bit from my trip to Japan, I waited until March to tackle Kauri Cliffs. Having been to New Zealand before, I looked forward to returning. During my previous visit, I had greatly enjoyed the scenery and the people. My latest trip started with a quick flight from San Francisco to Los Angeles, followed by a night flight to Auckland. During the flight from San Francisco to L.A., one of my fingers caught the sharp edge of a passing beverage cart. I was left with a deep cut that began to bleed profusely. It was the O'Hare incident all over again. Covering the cut with wet and dry napkins, I began to wonder if I would possibly need stitches. I also began thinking about my trip. Would I even be able to swing a golf club after the long flight to New Zealand? After landing in L.A., I did some further examining and wrapped the finger up as well as I could. Before wrapping it up, though, I purchased a nip of Jack Daniels whisky, which I poured on the wound as a sterilizer. I had to march on. The quest was nearly over. I couldn't stop now just because of a cut.

The following morning, I was in Auckland. My finger already looked a bit better. I was off to Kauri Cliffs Golf Club on the northern tip of New Zealand's east coast. One of New Zealand's newest courses, Kauri Cliffs was developed by American Julian Robertson, a New Yorker who made his fortune on Wall Street. After its completion, it took only three years for the course to achieve world-ranking status.

It was winter at home but summer in New

Zealand, providing me with perfect weather. Along with getting in my round at Kauri Cliffs, I ventured south to get in a round at another one of the Kiwis' newest courses—Cape Kidnappers. At the time of my visit, Cape Kidnappers had just recently opened. Like Kauri Cliffs, it is another majestic Julian Robertson course along the coast. Cape Kidnappers is so great, in fact, that when the rankings came out in the fall of 2005, it instantly cracked the Top 100.

After Cape Kidnappers, it was time to head home. While the trip was brief, the old saying *"Veni, Vidi, Vici"* ("I came, I saw, I conquered") came to my mind. There was only one last course left on my list—Augusta National Golf Club.

During the last two years, I had at one time or another networked my way into having eight possible connections that could help me find a way to get onto Augusta

---

One Man's Opinion

Best New Course
Kauri Cliffs
A great newcomer

Best Unranked Course
Cape Kidnappers
Not ranked, but will be

Best Golf Experience
Augusta National
Course, tradition, venue

Best Groomed Course
Augusta National
Two weeks after the Masters

Best Fairways
Augusta National
Two weeks after the Masters

Most Secure Course
Augusta National
Like a military base

Best Caddie
Ron McMahel,
Augusta National
The best

Hardest Course
to Get On
Augusta National
Good luck

National. By the time I got back from New Zealand, I had a mere three. One was an executive with a major golf resort, while the other was a combination of two close friends, Steve Munkdale and Jim Young, the "Big Blue" who had earlier helped me at Crystal Downs. Jim had tried for eight months to convince a friend of his who had a friend who was a member at Augusta. He had told me that he kept trying, but to no avail. Along with simply getting on, I had to remember that Augusta National has a schedule itself. Each year, the course closes from the end of May to the beginning of October, making May 31 the last tee-time for me to beat the new rankings.

Feeling as if I were so close yet so far away, I got my break when Steve called me in early April to tell me that he and Jim Young had made it happen. Their friend's friend had set up a tee-time for April 26, a mere month before the course would shut down for the summer. My instant reaction was exhilaration. I finally had a tee-time at Augusta, my 100th course, and the course where I precisely wanted to complete my quest.

My Augusta plan would revolve around a few days. After landing in Atlanta, I would head to Kiawah Island in neighboring South Carolina for a sort of Augusta National tune-up. I got in my round at Kiawah Island and headed straight back to Augusta to get in as much rest as possible in anticipation of my next day's play at the home of the Masters. That night, I went back over my notes on the course. I had been studying the yardage book for Augusta National for days and kept replaying holes in my head. I wanted my quest to finish on a high note.

The morning of my scheduled round at Augusta National Golf Club, I arrived outside the gates an hour early. At the main entrance, a security guard came out and asked my name. He told me who my member-host was but politely explained that I could not enter the grounds until he arrived. I was told to park across the street in a vacant shopping center while I waited.

During my wait, the weather turned sour. The forecast had called for showers, and the rain began dropping. Already nervous and excited, I worried and worried about the rain. What if I was rained out? When would I ever be back?

Finally, my host Fleming Norvell arrived and ushered me and another guest down famed Magnolia Lane towards the main clubhouse. We parked in front of the driving range. As soon as my car pulled in, my designated caddie named Ron was there to greet me, take my bag, and lead me to the range. The sun, whose rays had peeked through the clouds only moments earlier, gave way again to light drizzle but with every one of my steps, the caddie made sure I was dry under his umbrella. I was in!

After warming up on the range, we proceeded through the locker room to a large area near the first tee where all foursomes and their caddies gather before hitting the course. Because the Masters had just recently been held at Augusta, the grandstands and leaderboards were still standing. The sights themselves were incredible. Then, just before being told that our foursome was next on the tee, an impeccably dressed young man appeared from the clubhouse headed in our direction. When he got to us, he asked if I was Mr. Wentz, to which I replied, "Yes." I was then handed a scorecard with a note attached. Looking at the note, it said, "To Dad and Grandpa. Congratulations on playing No.100 and enjoy your round: Love, Brad and the Grandkids." It was from my son. What a nice way to start my round. I was nearly brought to tears. I showed the note to my host, who after reading it also nearly got teary-eyed and said, "Leon, you can lead off."

My first drive of the day wasn't very long, but I found the center of the fairway. My member-host and the other two members of our foursome also hit shots straight down the middle. As we walked down the fairway at No.1, I got to know a little bit more about the men I was playing with. My member-host, Fleming Norvell, had been a longtime member at Augusta. My contact David Chapman, who was a good friend of Fleming's, was a golf course developer from Palm Springs. The final player was a physician who was a member at Pine Valley. They all knew why I was there.

As we played on, the weather kept changing. One hole it would be rain, the next drizzle, the next sun. In the back of my mind, I just kept hoping that we would be able to finish. Along with worrying about the weather, I kept thinking about all of the great players who had walked the same fairways and putted the same greens in the previous two weeks. As we came up the hill to the green at No.9,

I had a perfect view of the clubhouse, the Butler Cabin, Eisenhower's house and Bobby Jones's one-time house.

Thanks to Ron, many of those images were captured on my digital camera. After No.9, I realized the course set-up. Amazingly, the pin locations were all the same ones used on Sunday during the Masters. The experience just kept getting better and better.

Though the rain was still drizzling a bit, on Hole No.11, I managed to card a par after hitting a solid drive and a nice approach. Next up was Hole No.12, the famous par-three that features a shot over Rae's Creek. On the tee, I asked Ron how I should play the hole to which he said, "Go for the pin." I did, but my first shot landed in the creek. Minutes later at the drop zone, I asked Ron for advice again. "Just relax and follow through with your lob wedge." Standing over my ball, I did just that, landing my third shot to within four feet from the pin. From there, I putted in for a bogey. Of course, things could have been much worse.

On the par-five 13th, the final hole of Amen Corner, I hit a short but straight drive. From there, I played short to avoid the creek that protects the green. Again, I had to hit another lob wedge, which again found the green. I went on to two-putt, carding yet another par. Overall, I had played the infamous Amen Corner to the tune of 1-over par! Not the kind of score that would earn me a Green Jacket, but not bad for a 67-year-old Augusta rookie who swings from the wrong side.

Later, as we got to the tee box at No.16, the weather seemed to finally break. The rain and drizzle were suddenly gone. Only a few days earlier, the Golf Gods had seemed to shine on Tiger Woods when he made his miraculous chip shot at No. 16 to help knock off Chris DeMarco to win the 2005 Masters. Now, it was my turn. As I stood in the tee box area, my mind began racing. Like Tiger, I had about 150 yards to the green and, of all things, I faced the same pin placement. After quickly conferring with Ron, I opted to go with a 7-iron that went straight for the back-right portion of the severely sloping green before landing in a greenside bunker at a 4 o'clock position. I hit my ball from the bunker to a point above and to the right of the pin, to a 1 o'clock position. After landing it made a left turn and rolled down past the cup and toward the water. I made bogie. It was at that moment that I realized how incredible Tiger's shot really was. It was literally a one-in-a-thousand chance. On that green, making a chip shot from off the green? There's no way! Yet Tiger had somehow made it happen.

The skies now clear, we later arrived at the tee box for Hole No.18. One more hole and my quest was complete! Through my years of watching the Masters, I always remembered the narrow gap through the trees where one was to hit a tee shot. Of course, the member's tee blocks were up, about an 85-yard difference, but it was still a challenging shot. My drive hit the middle of the fairway. From there, I looked to reach the green but instead found the bunker on the right-side portion of the green.

As we walked up to the green, our group was being serenaded by other members and their caddies. Word had apparently gotten around regarding my quest.

As I stood in the bunker, I soaked it in and surveyed my shot. I, of course, wanted to get out of the bunker and on the green, but I also wanted my ball to avoid landing down in the deep collection area that existed about 10 feet from that day's pin placement. After a quick swipe, I was out but my ball ran further than I wanted. I was off the green laying three. On my next shot, I bumped the ball into the slope with an 8-iron and watched the ball settle three feet below the cup. I was perhaps one putt away from finishing my quest.

With my knees knocking a bit, Fleming went to the cup and stood over it, forming a "V." "There is an unwritten rule here at Augusta National that says if you are finishing your last hole on your 100th course, you are not allowed to double bogey. Leon, I know you are nervous and thinking about a photo of some type. Well, here is what we'll do. Ron (my caddie), you stand over there and take the photo with Leon's camera. When Leon putts, I will stand over the cup with my caddie behind me with the pin and the Masters' scoreboard in the background." Ron had my camera out, ready to capture the final stroke. After a quick laugh, I stood over my putt and took a good look. A stroke later without the help of Fleming's feet, I was in. The quest was over!

Afterwards, we all shook hands, and I got more

than a few pats on the back. I immediately thanked my foursome and Ron, who had been so patient with me. Following the accolades, we all went directly to the clubhouse for lunch and a celebratory drink. There I was greeted by handshakes from the bartenders and waiters. During my walk to the clubhouse, I turned around and took another look at the green on No.18. I had really done it! I had completed my quest.

We celebrated for an hour or so at a table adjacent to an oil painting of the legendary Bobby Jones, and then I was on my way again, this time heading home for good. As I pulled out of Augusta National, I wanted to cry. It had been a truly great journey.

I had done it—from Pebble Beach to Augusta. For eight years, it was the time of my life.

The Top 100
2003-2005
(Golf Magazine)

COURSE	LOCATION	ARCHITECT(S)
1. Pine Valley	Clementon, NJ	Crump/Colt 1918
2. Cypress Point	Pebble Beach, CA	MacKenzie 1928; Egan
3. Muirfield	Gullane, Scotland	T. Morris, 1891; Colt, Simpson
4. Shinnecock Hills	Southampton, NY	Flynn, 1931
5. Augusta National	Augusta, GA	MacKenzie/Jones, 1932
6. St. Andrews (Old)	St. Andrews, Scotland	16th century
7. Pebble Beach	Pebble Beach, CA	Neville/Grant, 1919; Egan
8. Royal Melbourne (Composite)	Melbourne, Australia	MacKenzie/Russell, 1926
9. Pinehurst No.2	Pinehurst, NC	D.Ross, 1935
10. Royal County Down	Newcastle, Northern Ireland	T.Morris, 1889; Dunn, Vardon
11. Sand Hills	Mullen, NE	Coore/Crenshaw, 1995
12. Royal Portrush (Dunluce)	Portrush, Northern Ireland	Colt, 1929
13. Ballybunion (Old)	Ballybunion, Ireland	Murphy, 1906; Simpson, Gourlay
14. Merion (East)	Ardmore, PA	H.Wilson, 1912
15. Oakmont	Oakmont, PA	Fownes, 1903
16. Royal Dornoch	Dornoch, Scotland	T. Morris, 1886; Sutherland, Duncan
17. Turnberry (Alisa)	Turnberry, Scotland	P. M. Ross, 1906
18. Winged Foot (West)	Mamaroneck, NY	Tillinghast, 1923
19. Pacific Dunes	Bandon, OR	Doak, 2001
20. National	Southampton, NY	Macdonald, 1911
21. Kingston Heath	Cheltenham, Australia	Soutar, 1925; MacKenzie
22. Seminole	North Palm Beach, FL	D. Ross, 1929; D. Wilson
23. Prairie Dunes	Hutchinson, KS	Maxwell, 1935
24. Crystal Downs	Frankfort, MI	MacKenzie/Maxwell, 1929

COURSE	LOCATION	ARCHITECT(S)
25. Oakland Hills (South)	Bloomfield Hills, MI	D. Ross, 1917; R. T. Jones, Sr.
26. Carnoustie (Championship)	Carnoustie, Scotland	Robertson, 1842; T. Morris, Park, Braid
27. San Francisco	San Francisco, CA	Tillinghast, 1915
28. Royal Birkdale	Southport, England	Lowe, 1889; Hawtree/Taylor
29. Fishers Island	Fishers Island, NY	Raynor, 1917
30. Bethpage (Black)	Farmingdale, NY	Tillinghast, 1936; Rees Jones
31. Chicago	Wheaton, IL	Macdonald, 1895; Raynor
32. Royal St. George's	Sandwich, England	Purves, 1887; MacKenzie, Pennik, Steel
33. The Country Club (Championship)	Brookline, MA	Campbell, 1895; Flynn, Rees Jones
34. Casa de Campo (Teeth of the Dog)	La Romana, Dom. Republic	P. Dye, 1971
35. Hirono	Kobe, Japan	Allison, 1932
36. Riviera	Pacific Palisades, CA	Thomas/Bell, 1926; T. Fazio, Crenshaw/Coore
37. Muirfield Village	Dublin, OH	Nicklaus/Muirhead, 1974
38. Royal Troon (Old)	Troon, Scotland	Fernie, 1878; Braid
39. Olympic Club (Lake)	San Francisco, CA	Reid, 1917; Whiting, R.T. Jones Sr.
40. Portmarnock	Portmarnock, Ireland	G. Ross/Pickeman, 1894; Hawtree
41. Southern Hills	Tulsa, OK	Maxwell, 1935
42. Oak Hill (East)	Rochester, NY	D. Ross, 1926; R. T. Jones Sr, G and T. Fazio
43. New South Wales	La Perouse, Australia	MacKenzie, 1928
44. Sunningdale (Old)	Sunningdale, England	W.Park, 1901; Colt
45. Baltusrol (Lower)	Springfield, NJ	Tillinghast, 1922; R.T. Jones Sr.
46. Woodhall Spa	Woodhall Spa, England	Vardon, 1905; Colt, Hotchkin, Hutchison
47. Morfontaine	Senlis, France	Simpson, 1927
48. The Golf Club	New Albany, OH	P.Dye, 1967
49. Kauri Cliffs	Kaeo, New Zealand	Harmon, 2000
50. Royal Adelaide	Adelaide, Australia	Gardiner, 1904; MacKenzie

COURSE	LOCATION	ARCHITECT(S)
51. Shoreacres	Lake Bluff, IL	Raynor, 1919
52. Medinah (No.3)	Medinah, IL	Bendelow, 1928; Collis, Rulewich, Rees Jones
53. Whistling Straits (Straits)	Haven, WI	P. Dye, 1998
54. Royal Lytham and St. Annes	Lytham St. Annes, England	Lowe, 1886
55. Garden City	Garden City, NY	Emmet, 1898; Travis
56. Loch Lomond	Luss, Scotland	Weiskopf/Moorish, 1994
57. TPC at Sawgrass (Stadium)	Ponte Vedra Beach, FL	D. Ross, 1917; R. T. Jones Sr. P. Dye, 1981
58. Inverness	Toledo, OH	D. Ross, 1919; G. and T. Fazio, Hills
59. Los Angeles (North)	Los Angeles, CA	Thomas, 1921
60. Maidstone	East Hampton, NY	W. and J. Park, 1891; Tucker
61. Quaker Ridge	Scarsdale, NY	Tillinghast, 1926; R. T. Jones Sr.
62. Ganton	Ganton, England	T. Dunn, 1891; Colt, Cotton
63. Camargo	Cincinnati, OH	Raynor, 1921
64. Highlands Links	Ingonish Beach, Nova Scotia, Canada	Thompson, 1935; Cooke
65. Kingsbarns	St. Andrews, Scotland	Phillips, 1999
66. Winged Foot (East)	Mamaroneck, NY	Tillinghast, 1923
67. Harbour Town	Hilton Head Island, SC	P. Dye/Nicklaus, 1969
68. Cabo del Sol (Ocean)	Los Cabos, Mexico	Nicklaus, 1994
69. Somerset Hills	Bernardsville, NJ	Tillinghast, 1917
70. Durban Hotchkin	Durban, South Africa	Waters/Waterman, 1922;
71. Scioto	Columbus, OH	D. Ross, 1916; D. Wilson
72. Royal Liverpool	Hoylake, England	G. Morris/Chambers, 1869; Pennink
73. Lahinch	Lahinch, Ireland	T. Morris, 1893; Gibson, MacKenzie
74. Bandon Dunes	Bandon, OR	Kidd, 1999
75. Naruo	Osaka, Japan	Crane, 1904; Alison
76. Cruden Bay	Cruden Bay, Scotland	Fowler/Simpson, 1926
77. Valderrama	Sotogrande, Spain	R. T. Jones Sr., 1975
78. Wentworth (West)	Virginia Water, England	Colt/Morrison, 1924
79. Kiawah Island (Ocean)	Kiawah Island, SC	P. Dye, 1991
80. Kawana (Fuji)	Kawana, Japan	Alison/Fujita, 1936

COURSE	LOCATION	ARCHITECT(S)
81. Spyglass Hill	Pebble Beach, CA	R. T. Jones Sr., 1975
82. Walton Heath (Old)	Tadworth, England	Fowler, 1904
83. World Woods (Pine Barrens)	Brooksville, FL	T. Fazio, 1993
84. Ocean Forest	Sea Island, GA	Rees Jones, 1995
85. Valley Club of Montecito	Santa Barbara, CA	MacKenzie/Hunter, 1928
86. Congressional (Blue)	Bethesda, MD	Emmet, 1924; R. T. Jones Sr., Rees Jones
87. Peachtree	Atlanta, GA	R. T. Jones Sr./Bobby Jones, 1948
88. Wade Hampton	Cashiers, NC	T. Fazio, 1987
89. Shadow Creek	North Las Vegas, NV	T. Fazio, 1989
90. Cherry Hills	Cherry Hills Village, CO	Flynn, 1923
91. Baltimore (Five Farms East)	Lutherville, MD	Tillinghast, 1926; Silva
92. Yeamans Hall	Hanahan, SC	Raynor, 1925
93. El Saler	Valencia, Spain	Arana, 1967
94. Homestead (Cascades)	Hot Springs, VA	Flynn, 1923
95. St. George's	Etobicoke, Ontario, Canada	Thompson, 1929; Robinson
96. The Honors Course	Ooltewah, TN	P. Dye, 1984
97. East Lake	Atlanta, GA	Bendelow, 1910; D. Ross, Cobb, Rees Jones
98. European Club	Brittas Bay, Ireland	Ruddy, 1992
99. Paraparaumu Beach	Paraparaumu, New Zealand	Russell, 1949
100. Colonial	Fort Worth, TX	Bredemus, 1935; Maxwell

The
World's Perfect Course
One Man's View of the Best Golf Holes

PAR	HOLE	YARDS	COURSE	LOCATION
3	15	139	Cypress Point	California
3	13	159	Muirfield	Scotland
3	11	158	Shinnecock Hills	New York
3	12	155	Augusta National	Georgia
4	7	470	European Club	Ireland
4	17	461	St Andrews (Old)	Scotland
4	3	425	Oakmont	Pennsylvania
4	8	431	Pebble Beach	California
4	8	430	Prairie Dunes	Kansas
4	6	450	Royal Melbourne	Australia
4	10	440	Naruo	Japan
4	10	311	Riviera	California
4	17	333	Kauri Cliffs	New Zealand
4	13	448	Pine Valley	New Jersey
5	3	513	Durban	South Africa
5	13	560	Loch Lomond	Scotland
5	13	510	Augusta National	Georgia
5	1	600	Spyglass Hill	California
72		6993		

Timeline

1985—Pebble Beach, Spyglass Hill

1987—Olympic Club (Lake), Cypress Point, Colonial

1993—St. Andrews (Old), Cruden Bay, Royal Dornoch, Muirfield

1994—Royal Portrush (Dunluce), Royal County Down, Ballybunion (Old), Lahinch, Portmarnock

* 1997—Royal St. George's, Wentworth (West), Royal Lytham and St. Annes, Carnoustie (Championship), Turnberry (Ailsa), Royal Birkdale, Royal Liverpool

1998—Loch Lomond, Royal Troon (Old), Los Angeles (North), San Francisco

1999—Sunningdale (Old), Walton Heath (Old), Woodhall Spa, Ganton, Merion (East), Oakmont, The Golf Club

2000—New South Wales, Royal Adelaide, Kingston Heath, Royal Melbourne, Paraparaumu, Valderrama

2001—Shadow Creek, Maidstone, Shinnecock Hills, Pacific Dunes, Bandon Dunes, Baltusrol (Lower), National, Bethpage (Black), Winged Foot (West), Quaker Ridge

2002—Casa de Campo, Seminole, World Woods (Pine Barrens), Harbour Town, Kiawah Island (Ocean), Pinehurst No.2, TPC at Sawgrass (Stadium), Kingsbarns, Valley Club of Montecito, Morfontaine, Winged Foot (East), Garden City, East Lake, Peachtree, Riviera

2003—Crystal Downs, Whistling Straits, Medinah (No.3), Chicago, Shoreacres, Fishers Island, The Country Club, Oak Hill (East), Somerset Hills, Pine Valley, Congressional (Blue), Homestead (Cascades), The Honors Course, Wade Hampton, Southern Hills, Prairie Dunes, Cherry Hills

2004—Cabo del Sol (Ocean), El Saler, European, Durban, Baltimore (Five Farms East), Inverness, Oakland Hills, Muirfield Village, Scioto, Camargo, Highlands Links, St. George's, Sand Hills, Yeamans Hall, Ocean Forest, Naruo, Hirono, Kawana (Fuji)

2005—Kauri Cliffs, Augusta National

"Official" quest to play World's Top 100 Courses begins.

170

Acknowledgments

Doug Adams (California)
Adventures in Golf
   (New Hampshire)
Kathy Balderstrom
   (New York)
William Balderstrom
   (New York)
Jean Claude Benoist-Lucy
   (France)
Bill Beasley (California)
Mike Benjamin (Missouri)
Joseph Bettendorf (Ohio)
Bruce Black (California)
David Buoncristiani (California)
Brad Burris (North Carolina)
Timothy Cambias (Georgia)
Floyd Carley (California)
Michael Chadsey (Canada)
David Chapman (California)
Davis Clayson (Massachusetts)
Jack Coan (California)
Mike Coyles (Illinois)
Gordon Dalgleish (Georgia)
Jamie Daugherty (Michigan)
Tim Davis (Illinois)
Robin Faisant (California)
Bill Finestone (California)
Walter Forbes (Connecticut)
Bob Ford (Pennsylvania)
Jamie Gardner (Scotland)
Kenneth Gestal (Connecticut)
Steve Glossinger (Maryland)
Sidney Goodwin (Maryland)
A.J. Grymes (New Jersey)
Ken Hamill (New Hampshire)
Dennis Hansen (Minnesota)
RJ Harper (California)
Peggy Hart (Arizona)
Bill Hopkins (California)
James Howard (Georgia)

Ed Ingle (Tennessee)
Robbie Johnson
   (South Carolina)
Ralph Jones III (Connecticut)
Sieshi Jiromaru (Japan)
Iqbal Kahn (South Africa)
Shigiki Kanao (Japan)
Michael Kapland (Tennessee)
Irene Khatter (Canada)
Kiwi Golf (New Zealand)
Greg Kopan (Ohio)
Scott Lewis (California)
John Lister (Australia)
Loch Lomond Golf Club
   (Scotland)
James Lucius (California)
Malcom MacColl
   (Massachusetts)
Dr. Devinder Marrgat (Ohio)
Dr. Hewitt Mattox (Georgia)
William McCarren (Colorado)
Kathleen McDonald (Ohio)
Merrick McQuilling (New York)
Mark Michaud (New York)
Gray Mills (Texas)
Jay Milone (Georgia)
Mike Moore (South Africa)
Steve Munkdale (California)
Rob Murphy (New York)
John K. Nelson (Ohio)
Fleming Norvell (Georgia)
Tommy Parrish (South Carolina)
David Patterson (England)
Pebble Beach Company
   (California)
Michael Peck (Kansas)
David Pickett (New York)
Craig Plummer (Ohio)
Rick Purdy (California)
Chris Roderick (California)

Bill Rubinstein (Canada)
Scott Russell (Georgia)
John Ryan (New York)
Daisuke Saji (Japan)
Steve Schroeder (California)
George P. Schultz (California)
Tom Simmons (California)
Pat Sinclair (California)
Bill Smith (Georgia)
Bill Smith Jr. (Georgia)
Peter C. Smith (Maryland)
Scott Smith (New Jersey)
Paul Spengler (California)
Jim Stark (Georgia)
Morgan Stark (New York)
William Svoboda (California)
John Terry-Lloyd (South Africa)
James Thorne (Georgia)
Robert Thomas (Canada)

UCLA Athletic Department
(California)
United States Golf Association
(New Jersey)
Paul Walker (New Zealand)
Clark Wangaard (Illinois)
Brad Wentz (California)
Craig Wentz (California)
Julie Wentz (California)
Bob Wilson (California)
Dr. Charles Young (California)
Glen Young (Texas)
Jim Young (California)
John Youngscape (Nebraska)
Sandy Zahn (Illinois)
Tom Zammitt (Kansas)
Frank Zinn (Michigan)
Eugene Zuriff (New York)

Facts and Figures

11 courses lost because of ranking changes

Eight-year journey

(1997-2005)

326,000 miles covered

Five continents

14 countries

22 states

136 enablers worldwide

62 domestic courses

38 overseas courses

33 trips overall

100-plus cases of fine California vintage wines shipped
(when allowed by law) to each host as a thank-you along with
an invitation to be my guest at a West Coast course

Index

Index